NURSING FOR A MULTI-ETHNIC SOCIETY

'RACE', HEALTH AND SOCIAL CARE

Series editors:

Dr Waqar I.U. Ahmad, Head of Research Unit on Ethnicity and Social Policy, Department of Social and Economic Studies, University of Bradford.

Professor Charles Husband, Professor of Social Analysis and Associate Head, Research Unit on Ethnicity and Social Policy, Department of Social and Economic Studies, University of Bradford.

Minority ethnic groups now constitute over 5 per cent of the UK population. While research literature has mushroomed on the one hand in race and ethnic relations generally, and on the other in clinical and epidemiological studies of differences in conditions and use of health and social services, there remains a dearth of credible social scientific literature on the health and social care of minority ethnic communities. Social researchers have hitherto largely neglected issues of 'race' and ethnicity, while acknowledging the importance of gender, class and, more recently, (dis)ability in both the construction of and provision for health and social care needs. Consequently the available social science texts on health and social care largely reflect the experiences of the white population and have been criticized for marginalizing black people.

This series aims to provide an authoritative source of policy relevant texts which specifically address issues of health and social care in contemporary multi-ethnic Britain. Given the rate of change in the structure of health and social care services, demography and the political context of state welfare there is a need for a critical appraisal of the health and social care needs of, and provision for, the minority ethnic communities in Britain. By the nature of the issues we will address, this series will draw upon a wide range of professional and academic expertise, thus enabling a deliberate and necessary integration of theory and practice in these fields. The books will be inter-disciplinary and written in clear, non-technical language which will appeal to a broad range of students, academics and professionals with a common interest in 'race', health and social care.

Current and forthcoming titles

Waqar I.U. Ahmad and Karl Atkin: *'Race' and Community Care*
Kate Gerrish, Charles Husband and Jennifer Mackenzie: *Nursing for a Multi-ethnic Society*
Elizabeth N. Anionwu: *The Politics of Sickle Cell and Thalassaemia – 20 years on*
Lena Robinson: *Interracial Communication and Social Work Practice*
J. Owusu-Bempah and Dennis Howitt: *Professional Abuse of Black Childhood*

NURSING FOR A MULTI-ETHNIC SOCIETY

Kate Gerrish, Charles Husband and Jennifer Mackenzie

Open University Press
Buckingham · Philadelphia

Open University Press
Celtic Court
22 Ballmoor
Buckingham
MK18 1XW

and

1900 Frost Road, Suite 101
Bristol, PA 19007, USA

First Published 1996

A catalogue record of this book is available from the British Library

ISBN   0 335 19615 2 (pb)   0 335 19616 0 (hb)

Library of Congress Cataloging-in-Publication Data
Gerrish, Kate, 1955–
    Nursing for a multi-ethnic society/Kate Gerrish, Charles Husband, Jennifer Mackenzie.
        p.   cm. — (Race, health, and social care)
    Includes bibliographical references and index.
    ISBN 0–335–19616–0 (hb). — ISBN 0–335–19615–2 (pbk.)
    1. Nursing—Social aspects. 2. Minorities—Medical care—United States. 3. Nursing—Study and teaching. 4. Minorities in nursing—United States. I. Husband, Charles. II. Mackenzie, Jennifer. 1958– . III. Title. IV. Series.
    RT86.5.G47 1996
    362.1.'73'08693—dc20   96-24395
                                                                         CIP

Typeset by Graphicraft Typesetters Ltd, Hong Kong
Printed in Great Britain by Biddles Ltd, Guildford and King's Lynn

Contents

Foreword

The English National Board is delighted to agree the publication of this very important report through Open University Press and welcomes the opportunity to make the results of commissioned research and the implications for education and practice widely available to policy makers, managers, practitioners and researchers.

The findings which emerged from this research will enable professional and academic groups involved in the delivery of health care to use evidence-based findings to plan and implement significant change in nursing, midwifery and health visiting education and practice. These findings are also of relevance to other health care disciplines and multicultural groups involved in health care delivery.

The Board is undertaking work, based on these findings and recommendations, to develop its educational policy and standards for professional education, and in doing so, hopes that all those involved in education, practice and policy making will work together in partnership to improve health care practice.

Maureen Theobald
Chairman
English National Board

Jeff Thompson
Chairman
Research and Development Group
English National Board

Preface

On behalf of the Research and Development Group of the English National Board, I am delighted to take this opportunity to congratulate the research team on the completion of a very exciting project which will make an enormous contribution to our understanding of education for practice in a multicultural society.

The Steering Group which supported the research team throughout the two-year project is also to be thanked for the time and expertise which was given unstintingly, and which made such a significant contribution. The R&D Group describes the role of the Steering Group as a group of 'critical friends', and true to the spirit of reflective practitioners, the team and the group related as peers engaged in stimulating debate throughout this exciting project.

It has been the policy of the Board, in the recent commissioning process, to encourage multidisciplinary research teams. This team has provided the evidence that researchers from different academic and professional backgrounds enrich each other, and the outcomes of the research.

Sonia Crow
Assistant Director for Educational Policy (Research & Development)
English National Board

Acknowledgements

One of the most pleasant aspects of the work on this project has been the generous way in which so many people have given us their time, their ideas and the benefit of their knowledge and experience. Although they are too many to mention individually, we should like to convey our heartfelt thanks for the many and various ways in which they have contributed to the research. There are, however, a number of individuals whose contribution we would wish specifically to acknowledge.

We are grateful to the English National Board for Nursing, Midwifery and Health Visiting for providing the financial support to undertake this study, and to the members of the Steering Group for their support and guidance throughout the two years. Our special thanks go to the Chair, Waqar Ahmad, who, in carrying out his responsibilities with great sensitivity and humour, facilitated meetings which not only provided the opportunity for a critically constructive dialogue on the research process but also enabled the research team to return to the task in hand revitalized and full of enthusiasm. We would also wish to thank Sonia Crow, Assistant Director for Educational Policy (Research and Development) at the ENB for her support, advice and practical assistance throughout the project, which has proved to be a constant source of encouragement.

We are also enormously indebted to all those who participated in the research, especially the students and staff in the three case study locations who willingly gave of their time during a period of considerable organizational change. Finally, we should like to thank Yasmin Hussain, Tina Jones, Raymond Middleton and Lucy Thorne for their assistance in data preparation and analysis, Karen Chouhan and Annette Jinks for informing our thinking on curriculum audit and Wyn Healey and Chris Heathershaw for their secretarial support.

1

Introduction: the changing context of nursing and midwifery education

The background to the project

The National Health Service (NHS) was founded on the principle of providing appropriate and accessible health care services to the British population. Since its inception in 1948, changes in the demography of British society, in part brought about by post-war immigration and settlement in response to acute labour shortages and by more recent influxes of refugee populations, have created new and additional challenges to those involved in health care. Specifically, the need to respond to ethnic diversity in the provision of health care services, while previously occupying a marginalized position in health policy and service delivery, has come increasingly to the fore. In addition, there is a growing recognition of the inequities and inequalities evident in health and health care provision and how these may impact upon the experiences of minority ethnic communities, with the result that increasing attention is being paid to the need to provide services which avoid discrimination and promote equality of opportunity (Smaje 1995).

It is within the context of this increasing awareness of the need to develop health care services which are responsive to the needs of an ethnically diverse society that the English National Board for Nursing, Midwifery and Health Visiting (ENB) commissioned a two-year research project examining the preparation of nurses and midwives to work in a multi-ethnic context. This book provides an account of the project, the specific aim of which was to examine the extent to which pre-registration programmes of nursing and midwifery education prepare practitioners to meet the health care needs of minority ethnic communities. In this introductory chapter we provide a brief description of the context in which the research took place before moving on to give an overview of the research objectives and methods employed. In subsequent chapters, we provide a systematic account of the different stages of the research project and consider the implications arising from the findings for the future preparation of nurses and midwives for their role in contributing positively to health care in a multi-ethnic society.

As a research team we readily acknowledge that any research enterprise is influenced not only by those who engage directly in the research process, either as researchers or as subjects of the inquiry, but also by the context in which it takes place. On the one hand, our task was clearly defined within the confines of the project specification which had been drawn up by the commissioning body: we had been charged with the responsibility to examine the extent to which nurses and midwives are prepared to meet the health care needs of minority ethnic communities by examining pre-registration programmes of education in their broadest sense. This necessitated us determining the methodology by which we would seek to accomplish our task and then engaging with education institutions which provided such programmes in order to collect our data.

However, we were also acutely aware from the outset of the context in which the study was to be located and how this would impact upon all aspects of the research. We identified two interrelated dimensions to this context. The first concerned the need for us to seek to understand the *broader* context in which an examination of the ethnic related aspects of nursing and midwifery curricula needed to take place. Specifically, we recognized the central importance of appreciating the social and political significance of ethnicity within contemporary Britain, together with an understanding of the lived experiences of minority ethnic communities, particularly in relation to their experiences of health care. We also recognized that nursing and midwifery education does not take place in isolation but is heavily influenced by a wider health and education arena. In particular, we identified a need to take account of how both health and education policy impact upon the preparation of nurses and midwives to work in a multi-ethnic society. The second dimension related to a recognition of the need to take account of the *historical* context in which the study is located. Already, as we write up a research enterprise which has spanned two years, we recognize that time has moved on, and with it changes have occurred, not just within nursing and midwifery education, but also within the wider health care arena. Inevitably these changes have exerted some degree of influence on us not only in terms of how we have carried out the research, but also in respect of how we have interpreted our findings and the recommendations which have arisen subsequently.

In order to help the reader appreciate something of the context within which the research is located, we propose, by way of introduction, to summarize some of the key contextual issues which have influenced our thinking as we have taken forward the research. Specifically, we will focus on examining the changing context of nursing and midwifery education within the broader health and education arena in order to set the scene for our subsequent account of the research. We leave a detailed examination of ethnicity and the experiences of minority ethnic communities to Chapters 2 and 3.

The changing context of nursing and midwifery education

In recent years nursing and midwifery education has been subject to considerable change. The most significant of these changes has occurred as a result of the implementation of proposals for major reforms in pre-registration nurse education (United Kingdom Central Council (UKCC) 1986). The 'Project 2000' proposals, as they became known, were developed in response to a recognition that in the mid-1980s nurse education was failing to equip practitioners with the necessary knowledge and skills to provide appropriate health care into the 1990s and beyond, particularly in respect of responding to the changing health needs of the population and changes in the delivery of health care services. Project 2000 stressed the importance of basing nursing practice on a model of health as opposed to the existing disease orientation, and recognized the need for practitioners to be equipped with the necessary skills to practise in both institutional and community contexts. In order to achieve these intentions, a major revision of pre-registration nursing programmes of education ensued. In addition to substantial changes in curriculum content, there were also significant changes to the structure and standard of education programmes. As a result, the three-year programme is now divided into: an initial 18-month common foundation programme in which all students study collectively the knowledge base which underpins nursing practice and gain exposure to the full range of nursing specialisms; followed by an 18-month branch programme in which students pursue one particular nursing specialism, in adult, mental health, learning disabilities or children's nursing. Students who successfully complete a branch programme are then eligible for registration as a nurse with the United Kingdom Central Council for Nursing, Midwifery and Health Visiting (UKCC) in their particular specialism. In addition, the education reforms also brought about changes in the academic standing of pre-registration programmes, with the Diploma of Higher Education becoming the minimum qualification for registration as a nurse. While not subject to the same overtly radical change, pre-registration midwifery education has, by and large, followed a similar trajectory to nurse education, in that its primary focus has shifted to become clearly based on women's health needs. And in a similar vein to nursing, the minimum academic standard for pre-registration midwifery programmes has been set at diploma level.

In recent times the majority of nursing and midwifery education has been based within the NHS, although, since the 1960s, there has been a small but increasing number of universities which offer undergraduate pre-registration programmes; initially in nursing and more recently in midwifery. At the time of undertaking the study, the proportion of practitioners qualifying from degree programmes was small in comparison to diploma programmes. However, the acceptance of the Diploma of Higher Education as the minimum qualification for professional registration has led NHS colleges of nursing and midwifery to formalize links with higher education institutions in order to seek academic accreditation for their provision. This relationship with higher education has been further extended through the requirement for colleges to become fully integrated with higher education institutions. At the time of commencement of the research approximately 13 per cent of diploma level programmes were offered by universities, the remainder being based within NHS colleges who were making rapid progress towards integration, with the intention that this would be completed by April 1996. The fact that the study spanned a two-year period between January 1994 and December 1995 meant that we were engaging chiefly with NHS based colleges of nursing and midwifery which would no longer exist in the form in which they were examined by the time the report of the study would be published. In reflecting upon the peculiarities of this research situation, we are mindful of the implications that this has for any recommendations that arise from the study.

The particular knowledge and skills that nurses and midwives are required to possess upon registration are specified within the statutory instruments emanating from the Nurses, Midwives and Health Visitors Act 1979. An acknowledgement of the need for nurses to be prepared to meet the health care needs of minority ethnic communities was highlighted in the amendments made to the Act with the implementation of Project 2000 courses. Specifically, all nurses who complete such programmes should be able to demonstrate an 'appreciation of the influence of social, political and *cultural* factors in relation to health care' (Nurses, Midwives and Health Visitors (Registered Fever Nurses) Amendment Rules 1989: No 1456, Rule 18a (d)). The responsibility for ensuring that pre-registration programmes of nursing and midwifery education provide the opportunity for students to achieve the learning outcomes specified by the UKCC is conferred on the ENB. To this end, the ENB is responsible for granting professional accreditation of education programmes offered by institutions and, in discharging this responsibility, provides extensive policy guidelines on the approval of institutions and programmes, including details on curriculum methods and approaches (ENB 1993). However, in respect of preparing practitioners to meet the needs of minority ethnic communities, neither the ENB nor the UKCC provides much in the way of specific guidance on curriculum content. Rather, they provide more general guidance on the requirements for programmes to provide the opportunity for students to develop a *holistic* approach to care which reflects a multicultural society, and in order to achieve this, indicate a need to study relevant social and behavioural sciences which are seen to lead to an understanding of different cultures (ENB 1989; UKCC 1989). Beyond these general guidelines it is left to individual institutions to determine the exact curriculum content, methods and approaches to be incorporated within their programmes.

The ENB also specifies that programmes should equip students with the competencies to meet the needs of local populations. It follows that in parts of the country where there is considerable ethnic diversity the curriculum should reflect this. While this requirement appears commendable, the corollary is that it does allow the potential opportunity for programmes offered in areas where the population is less ethnically diverse to abdicate some responsibility for addressing ethnicity and its implications for health care practice. This directive also highlights something of a tension between training a workforce to meet local needs and equipping practitioners to work in different parts of the country, where the ethnic composition of local populations may be quite different.

Despite the directives from statutory bodies that educational programmes should equip practitioners with the necessary knowledge and skills to meet the needs of minority ethnic communities, there is little research upon which to base curriculum development. Although in recent years there has been a growing body of literature addressing the issues associated with nursing in a multi-ethnic society, and the implications this has for nursing and midwifery education, the majority of this work lacks any empirical basis. Much of it emanates from North America and has centred upon an interpretation of the interface of culture with nursing, drawing heavily upon Leininger's anthropologically based theory of transcultural nursing (Leininger 1978). In particular, authors have been keen to explore how an understanding of cultural diversity can lead to greater sensitivity on the part of the nurse in responding to the specific needs of patients from a different ethnic background to their own (DeSantis 1994), and there have been subsequent attempts to incorporate this thinking within educational developments in North America (Fulton 1985; Lynam 1992) and more recently in the UK (Dobson 1986; McGee 1992, 1994; Papadopoulos *et al.* 1994a, b). But as yet these initiatives lack systematic evaluation.

However, while we do not wish to negate the importance of responding to cultural diversity in professional practice, it is not in itself a sufficient response to meeting the health care needs of minority ethnic clients. Arguably, there is also a need to contextualize the health experiences of minority ethnic communities within the broader social and political arena and in particular to take account of the dynamics of disadvantage and discrimination which structure many aspects of the minority ethnic person's experience of everyday life (Culley 1996). To date, the nursing literature has largely ignored this dimension, but we will return to consider the implications for the nursing professions in subsequent chapters.

The broader health care context

Nursing and midwifery education itself cannot be viewed in isolation from the broader health care context. Students are being trained to assume future professional roles within the health services, and during the course of their programmes are exposed to health provision through practice experience. Inevitably, changes within the health care arena impact upon the preparation of nurses and midwives and it is to a brief consideration of these influences that we now turn.

Concomitant with the reforms in nursing and midwifery education have come radical reforms in health care. The NHS and Community Care Act 1990 signalled the formal adoption of the proposals for health service reform outlined in two separate White Papers: *Working for Patients* (Department of Health (DoH) 1989a) and *Caring for People* (DoH 1989b). A number of significant changes ensued, most notably the creation of an internal market within the health service, whereby commissioning authorities were charged with the responsibility of determining the health needs of local populations and then purchasing health care services accordingly. Initially, neither of the White Papers paid much overt attention to Britain's multi-ethnic society, but by implication, health service providers in areas where the local population was ethnically diverse were challenged to develop services which were responsive to the needs of the different minority ethnic communities and which provided for equality of access to health care provision. Arguably this should mean that the health care needs of minority ethnic communities are taken account of in strategic health planning, service provision commissioning and service delivery. However, there is a wealth of literature which indicates that the health care needs of minority ethnic communities are, to an extent, unmet. This is seen to be primarily owing to the marginalization of ethnic issues within the health policy agenda, with the consequent failure of services to meet the needs of minority ethnic communities. We refer readers to Ahmad (1993a) and Smaje (1995) for a detailed critique of this literature.

Perhaps as a consequence of these criticisms, there does appear to have been a recent attempt to address the previous marginalization of ethnic health issues within health policy by recognizing ethnic difference and attempting to tackle ethnic inequality (Ahmad 1992a). For example, a recognition within the Health of the Nation Strategy (DoH 1992) of the specific needs of minority ethnic communities (DoH 1993a), together with an emphasis in the Patient's Charter (DoH 1991) on responding to the 'religious and cultural beliefs' of clients, have been viewed as overdue indications that policy makers are beginning to address ethnic diversity (Johnson 1992). Indeed, the most recent report of the Chief Medical Officer (DoH 1995a) on the state of the public health asserts that the health of minority ethnic communities is designated a priority area by the Department of Health and an important consideration in the development of future health policy. However, although these developments provide a potential way forward it is as yet too early to evaluate what their impact might be on the nature and provision of health care for minority ethnic communities.

If these intentions are taken seriously, they have implications for the nature of pre-registration preparation of nurses and midwives as well as the continuing education of existing practitioners. To this end, the health service reforms have recognized the need to secure an appropriately skilled workforce in order to achieve its purposes and objectives (National Health Service Executive (NHSE) 1995) and acknowledged that in order to provide appropriate services in a multi-ethnic society, health care practitioners need to possess the requisite knowledge and skills to deliver care which is ethnically sensitive and non-discriminatory (Waldegrave 1992). Working Paper 10 (DoH 1989c) set out a framework for education and training in the health care sector to align it with the wider health service reforms. With the exception of a small number of undergraduate programmes funded through the Higher Education Funding Council for England (HEFCE), pre-registration nursing and midwifery education was, and indeed still is, contracted through Working Paper 10 arrangements. Regional health authorities (RHAs) were charged with the responsibility for identifying the level of demand for newly qualified practitioners in consultation with health service purchasers and providers and then commissioning education and training from education providers in both the NHS and higher education sectors. Although the main focus of the RHAs' activities has been on matching education contracts with workforce planning estimates, they have also developed an interest in the more strategic issues of health professional education and training to underpin their investment. Among these has been a concern to monitor the quality of the education and training they commission in respect of the extent to which it responds to the needs of the health service (Hilbourne *et al.* 1994).

From April 1996, RHAs began to transfer their educational commissioning responsibility to purchasing consortia comprising representatives from local health care purchasers and providers. Underpinning this move is an intention on the part of the government to develop an employer-led process for education commissioning which aims to take account of local needs, in terms of both the number of staff needed and the knowledge and skills required of health care practitioners to provide an appropriate service to local populations. Consortia have also been charged with the responsibility of improving the participation of minority ethnic people within the health professions and with strengthening the involvement of clients and lay carers in the development, management and evaluation of programmes of professional training (NHSE 1995). These responsibilities are likely to lead to a number of concerns that consortia may have as education commissioners in ensuring that education provision meets service needs, and highlight the significant position that health care purchasers and providers increasingly will occupy in influencing the future direction of nursing and midwifery education. This brings to the fore the need for nursing and midwifery education to be responsive in developing practitioners who are competent to practice in a multi-ethnic society.

An overview of the research process

The remainder of this book provides an account of the research we undertook in order to examine the extent to which pre-registration programmes of nursing and midwifery education equip practitioners to practice effectively within a multi-ethnic society. Specifically, we were required by the ENB to examine the ethnic-related content of curricula and their relevance to the health care needs of minority ethnic communities, together with the teaching and learning methods and approaches used in both classroom and practice settings. In order to consider the extent to which programmes prepared practitioners to meet the health care needs of minority ethnic communities, we sought to ascertain the perceptions of a range of interested parties: these included minority ethnic clients, students and their teachers, practitioners and managers in both education and service settings. Finally, we were also required by the ENB to examine the ethnic background of students entering pre-registration nursing and midwifery programmes.

Although we readily acknowledged the relevance of the research objectives to each of the branches of nursing, we chose to focus our attention on diploma level pre-registration programmes in adult and mental health nursing, in addition to midwifery. Our choice was in part influenced by a recognition that demographic changes are resulting in an increasingly elderly minority ethnic population who are likely to place new and additional demands upon those involved in adult nursing. In addition, we were acutely aware of the criticisms in the literature of the inadequacies of mental health provision provided to minority ethnic clients and recognized the central role that nurses should occupy in the future development of these services.

The remaining chapters of this report provide a detailed account of the different stages of the research, together with the implications of our findings for future education and practice.

In Chapter 2 we provide an introduction to the analysis of ethnic diversity in Britain. So that in later chapters readers may be able to develop their own perspectives on emerging responses to the health care needs of minority ethnic communities, the chapter then proceeds to offer a brief account of the development of different policy strategies towards managing ethnic diversity. It concludes with an exploration of the ways in which ethnic diversity may have implications for the nursing professions and provides an analysis of what may be involved in these professions moving towards appropriate modes of care in a multi-ethnic context.

Building upon the earlier exploration of ethnicity as a phenomenon in contemporary society and locating current attempts of contemporary social policy to respond to ethnic diversity within a critical historical perspective, Chapter 3 examines the user's experience of health care provision in general, and nursing and midwifery in particular. It provides a critical account of the literature in this area before moving on to present the qualitative data of personal experiences which were derived from interviews with minority ethnic service users. While this part of the study provides but a very limited snapshot of the experiences of minority ethnic service users, we offer it as a modest contribution to supporting the extant published literature in this area. The range of experiences of minority ethnic service users in receiving nursing and midwifery care also serves to make explicit and concrete the reality of health care in contemporary Britain; and underlines the expectation of appropriate professional preparation which all education institutions must acknowledge. In presenting the findings in this and subsequent chapters we have drawn directly upon the words of those whom we interviewed. Each extract has been allocated a reference number, which denotes the particular interviewee and the page and section of the interview transcript.

In order to gain an overview of the ethnic related content, together with the methods and approaches used in nursing and midwifery curricula, we undertook a survey by postal questionnaire of all institutions offering pre-registration diploma level programmes in adult nursing, mental health nursing and midwifery in England. Chapter 4 begins by providing an account of the methods used in this stage of the study. We then move on to consider the findings from the survey, which serve to provide a comprehensive account of the current variability of curricula and give an indication of the extent to which the programmes prepare practitioners to meet the health care needs of minority ethnic communities.

Building upon the data arising from the national survey, we then sought to undertake a more detailed in-depth analysis of nursing and midwifery programmes by carrying out case studies of a selection of education institutions. We chose three institutions that on the basis of the survey's findings, were seen to be making progress towards equipping practitioners with the necessary competencies to work in a multi-ethnic context. In Chapter 5 we outline the methods employed in this stage before moving on to present the data arising from focus group discussions with students, their teachers, mentors and assessors and newly qualified practitioners, together with individual interviews with education and service managers. These case studies provide a rich and varied account of the complexities of preparing practitioners for their role in a multi-ethnic society and highlight the interrelationship between curricula design and delivery and the organizational context in which education takes place.

Chapter 6 addresses the recruitment of minority ethnic persons into nursing and midwifery education. In order to set the context for an analysis of statistical data on the current national pattern of recruitment to the programmes with which the study is concerned, we begin by presenting an overview of the main issues to arise from a review of the literature and then consider some of the methodological problems inherent in the collection and interpretation of ethnic-related data. The analysis of statistical data is extended by a consideration of qualitative data derived from interviews with education and service managers in the case study institutions. This has served to provide some indicators as to the current position of the recruitment of minority ethnic students into nursing and midwifery education and also to provide a basis for monitoring future trends.

In Chapter 7, we draw together the main issues to arise from the findings of the different stages of the study by focusing on three overarching concerns, namely issues associated with curricula, practice experience and the recruitment and retention of minority ethnic students within the nursing professions. In discussing our conclusions, we recognize the complex and wide-ranging factors which impact upon the preparation of practitioners to function effectively in a multi-ethnic society. While some issues can be addressed by individuals at the level of curriculum design and delivery, others have more far-reaching implications and require changes in policy at institutional and national levels.

2

Ethnicity, the minority ethnic community and health care delivery

Introduction

This chapter examines the issue of ethnicity, and provides a basic introduction to the analysis of ethnic diversity in Britain. The purpose of this
introduction is to enable the reader to place the research findings into a
broader context. The response to the arrival and settlement of migrant
communities in Britain after the Second World War provides the framework within which contemporary 'race relations' are usually understood.
A core feature of this response was the belief that Britain had suddenly
become 'multi-ethnic', and that the host population had been faced with
the novel challenge of ethnic diversity. The first section of this chapter
demonstrates that this belief was based on a perverse understanding of our
national history. When the real ethnic diversity of British history is pointed
out, the invention of a British identity is revealed as being a particular
historical political project which has very real significance in contemporary
Britain. Thus the post-war response to the settlement of migrant workers
and to the development of minority ethnic communities has to be seen as
a part of the continuing process of the construction of British identity.
Nationalist sentiments have played a significant part in shaping the life
experience of minority ethnic communities in Britain, and have had an
impact in shaping the majority population's perception of the rights of
minority ethnic communities. It is argued that an adequate understanding
of contemporary responses to ethnic diversity must draw upon a knowledge of this broader history.

In order that in later chapters readers may be able to develop their own
perspectives on emerging responses to the health care needs of minority
ethnic communities, the chapter proceeds to offer a brief account of the
emergence of different policy strategies towards managing ethnic diversity
in Britain. The transition from policies of assimilation, to multiculturalism,
to anti-racism is sketched, and the complex coexistence of these models in

current social policy is discussed. This analysis of broad models of how multi-ethnic societies should manage the difference of experience and expectations between a variety of ethnic communities has important implications for an understanding of the range of responses to that diversity which may be demanded of practitioners; and of health and social care institutions.

In the next section the concept of ethnicity is explored in order to identify the ways in which ethnic diversity may have implications for the nursing professions. This section stresses the complexity of ethnic identities and begins to open up questions about how practitioners may negotiate their own ethnicity and that of their client. The broader relations of power between the majority ethnic community and members of minority ethnic communities is shown to have relevance for both interpersonal interaction and access to social and institutional resources. It is argued that ethnicity is not just a sense of who we are, but is also constructed through the ability to live that identity; to express it in our everyday life. This structural aspect of ethnicity has implications for both the construction of health needs and the possibility of providing appropriate health care.

Drawing upon these two prior sections, the final section provides an analysis of what may be involved in the nursing professions moving towards appropriate cultural care in a multi-ethnic context. The specific features of the cultural values and practices of particular ethnic communities constitute one challenge to providing appropriate care. However, it is argued that without the development of a general personal adaptability to inter-ethnic contacts, such culture specific knowledge is unlikely to be employed sensitively and appropriately. Additionally, it is argued that health care systems must show creative flexibility in responding to the health care needs of minority ethnic communities. In the evaluation of the research findings which follow, it would be most unfortunate if it was assumed that changing the competencies of individual practitioners was a sufficient response to the challenge of ethnic diversity faced by the nursing professions.

Building upon the analytic framework developed in this chapter, the following chapter then provides a concrete response to the theoretical and generalized analysis outlined here. It provides an introduction to the experience of minority ethnic service users' experience of nursing and midwifery care in contemporary England. In drawing on qualitative data of personal experience, it hopes to demonstrate the absolute necessity of addressing the issues raised in this chapter.

A necessary brief history

Constructing a national self-image

Within the broader concerns that the diversity of users should be recognized in the provision of health care, the particular needs of minority ethnic communities have in recent years been given a clear recognition. This of course has not always been so, and a 'colour-blind' approach to health care has historically been the corollary of national policies in determining the state's response to Britain's changing demography following post-war immigration and settlement. In order to understand this recent history it is appropriate, and necessary, that we should begin with an insight into the broader historical background. We should note that it has been a historical characteristic of the national government based in London to promote a conception of British national identity that was spuriously homogeneous. The invention of Britain as an imaginable collectivity owed much to an emphasis on a Protestant common identity in opposition to a Catholic Europe (Colley 1992). This fabrication of Britain also took place during a period of colonial expansion and imperial political self-aggrandizement in which persons in Africa and Asia constituted an alien *other* against whom Britons could rehearse conceptions of shared biology and culture (Kiernan 1969; Walvin 1971). And closer to home geographically, the Celtic identities of the Scots, Welsh and Irish had been suppressed in the essentially English construction of Britain (Hechter 1975), while through the latter part of the nineteenth century and into the twentieth century the Irish remained a highly significant outgroup in English politics and culture (Curtis 1968, 1971). And running through this historical construction of British identity, and those of its outgroups, ran the language of 'race' (Banton and Harwood 1975; Rich 1990). A belief in the scientific justification for the existence of distinct 'races', and for believing in the superiority of white, Anglo-Saxon Britons, played a powerful role in justifying oppression, and even near genocide. Despite the modern scientific rejection of such 'race' theory (Mason 1986), the idea of distinct 'races' continues in popular thought, and is currently sustained by ever evolving cultural and socio-biological speculation (Barker 1981; Husband 1987). Thus the common sense, taken-for-granted notion of British identity which was invoked in response to the post-war process of immigration was a political construction with a very particular history.

Not only was the deep-seated sense of shared English/British identity a product of an 'invention of tradition' (Hobsbawm and Ranger 1983) in which a common agenda of cultural symbols and institutions had been fabricated: the assumed relative homogeneity of the British in fact suppressed a history rich in diversity. The Romans, Angles, Saxons and Normans have all contributed to British history through invasion. And over the centuries successive movements of immigrants and refugees have provided further grist to the British mill: in the late seventeenth century, up to 100,000 Huguenots fled from France; in the mid-nineteenth century, famine in Ireland drove thousands of Irish into England and Scotland; and at the turn of the century, an estimated 120,000 European Jews entered Britain between 1875 and 1914 (Foot 1965; Holmes 1978). And should this account leave some with a conception that this history is at any rate a migration of 'Europeans' across borders, it should also be noted that there is a long history of Black settlement in Britain (Walvin 1973; Fryer 1984). Perhaps it is an indication of the success of the mythology of British homogeneity that the following observation would have little popular credibility in contemporary Britain: 'The British are clearly among the most ethnically composite of the Europeans' (Geipel 1969: 163).

Emerging perspectives for policy in multi-ethnic Britain

In coming to address the British response to post-war immigration one should at least start from a sense of the historical reality of British ethnic diversity, and of the ironically complementary history of the construction and defence of a homogenizing British identity. Perhaps this sensibility may make the initial response to the arrival of Afro-Caribbean and Asian migrants more intelligible. The assumption of governments throughout the 1950s and into the 1970s was that provided their children were given support with the English language in schools, the immigrant population would 'learn to become like us'; that is, they would be *assimilated*. The expectation that immigrant workers who arrived in Britain, and became the core of a number of settled minority ethnic communities within urban Britain, would give up their culture and ethnic identity in return for their resident rights here proved to be naive. This *assimilationist* model was based upon an inadequate understanding of the social psychology of group identity; and in particular of the resilience of ethnic identities in contexts where the minority community is marginalized and faces hostility (Tajfel 1978; Husband 1982). Additionally, assimilationist policies assumed that the 'newcomer' would be allowed to merge into the host society. However, the Afro-Caribbean and Asian migrants entering Britain in the 1950s and 1960s experienced very considerable hostility (Humphrey and John 1971; Studlar 1974). When a minority community begins to adopt the cultural practices of the dominant ethnic community and is still rejected by the majority population, then assimilation is hardly a viable political, or cultural, option. Given this scenario, it seems hardly surprising that the xenophobia and racism present in the majority population should have reinforced any tendency of the minority communities to attempt to retain their unique ethnic values and culture.

It is important for any understanding of the challenge facing contemporary nursing and midwifery to recognize that the resentment and hostility directed towards the developing minority ethnic communities in Britain in the 1960s and 1970s was not just spontaneous 'prejudice' on the part of members of the majority population. Certainly that did exist and was very significant; but it was the entry of 'race' into party politics which exacerbated this situation. As the major political parties sought to achieve an electoral gain through pandering to these prejudices, so too they progressively contributed to making ethnic diversity into a 'racial' political agenda (Miles and Phizacklea 1984; Solomos 1993). Consequently, Britain has developed social policies which have attempted to manage diversity in the interests of a majority self-consciously resentful of the demands of minority ethnic communities (Jenkins and Solomos 1989; Anthias and Yuval-Davis 1993).

Multiculturalism through the 1970s and into the 1980s has been such a policy. Responding to the failure of assimilation, multiculturalism emerged as a policy which allowed for the recognition of ethnic diversity in Britain. It offered cultural pluralism as a means of limiting the social upheaval generated by extremist racism, and it attempted to reclaim the British virtue of tolerance in the face of visible racial discrimination and continuing popular hostility towards members of minority ethnic communities. Regrettably, this focus upon culture allowed the majority institutions to locate their difficulties in meeting the assumed needs of minority communities as being within the minority culture. Whether in education (Stone 1981; Troyna and Williams 1986), probation and social work (Rooney 1987) or health care (Ahmad 1993b), minority ethnic communities were perceived to be responsible for their own failure to progress. Multiculturalism has provided a framework within which ethnic diversity may be recognized by policy makers; and respect for different cultures may be encouraged between individuals. It has, however, been severely criticized for its failure to address inequalities of power and resources between the majority and minority communities (Bourne 1980; Centre for Contemporary Cultural Studies (CCCS) 1982). This failure has, among other things, allowed the majority essentially to define the perceived characteristics of minority cultures, and to intervene in defining their needs; the rickets campaign being one such instance (Smaje 1995: Chapter 7). The majority's ethnicity has remained invisible. It is taken for granted as the norm; only other people are ethnic. Thus within multiculturalism the identity and needs of the minority ethnic communities have tended to be determined in a political process where *their* difference has been the perceived problem. Multiculturalism continues to be a much invoked concept, though one with increasingly disparate meanings and policy implications (Goldberg 1994).

Through the late 1970s and into the mid-1980s multiculturalism was critiqued by members of minority ethnic communities, who deeply resented its implicit paternalism, and by political analysts, who felt that it obscured the structural bases of inequality and the racist ideologies which replicated those processes of discrimination and exclusion that marginalized minority ethnic communities within Britain. Particularly after the major civil disturbances of the early 1980s (Kettle and Hodges 1982; Joshua and Wallace 1983), *anti-racist* strategies emerged as an alternative to multiculturalism. This model of recognizing the conflicts of interest within multi-ethnic Britain and of addressing systematic processes of inequality within British institutions was never widely acceptable. In focusing upon access to control over resources, and upon those locations in routine professional and institutional practices where discretionary power was exercised, this model rejected a simplistic equation of racism with prejudice. It developed the insights derived from the concept of *institutional racism* which had informed the 1976 Race

Relations Act, and made visible the uncomfortable truth that 'nice people' may be involved, through their routine professional practice, in generating discriminatory outcomes (see, for example, Williams 1985; Miles 1989). Politically, it drew upon more sophisticated analyses of racist discourse, which revealed the many ways in which minority ethnic communities may be defined as alien and threatening without resort to grossly explicit racist rhetoric (see, for example, Essed 1991; van Dijk 1991).

As a model for responding to the inequalities and discrimination within a multi-ethnic society, *anti-racism* was a direct challenge to those members of the indigenous dominant white community who felt comfortable with Britain's tolerant credentials. And it was an affront to those who felt that the interests of the dominant majority were being compromised by the demands of ungrateful minority ethnic communities. To a Conservative government that was promoting a robust philosophy of individual self-interest coupled with an explicit English nationalism, fused together as Thatcherism (Jessop *et al.* 1987), this model was intolerable. Anti-racism attracted a vehement onslaught from the British right wing (Murray and Searle 1989; Gordon 1990), with local authorities which had seemingly embraced it being targeted as 'looney left', and those within professional bodies who sought to embrace its insights being isolated. The recent experience within the Central Council for Education and Training in Social Work (CCETSW) is a good example (Jones 1993). This social work equivalent of the ENB over a number of years moved to develop an explicit anti-racist agenda within social work training (CCETSW 1991a, b, 1992). The impetus for this came from committed individuals within CCETSW and strong strands of support from disparate interests within social work (Husband 1994: Chapter 7). As Jones indicates, the momentum associated with this initiative was stalled by an orchestrated campaign within and without CCETSW.

Anti-racism as a model for policies in a multi-ethnic society, like multiculturalism before it, was never a homogeneous and systematized policy coherently shared among those who espoused it (Husband 1995). It attracted a wide range of critiques from many on the left and from minority ethnic communities who found it strong on rhetoric and weak on delivering change (for example, Gilroy 1990; Troyna 1992). However, the reaction against anti-racist policies from the political right has been very successful and the current policy environment in response to the challenge of multi-ethnic Britain is confused. At a governmental level, the promotion of English ethnicity as being synonymous with British national identity continues. The 1988 Education Reform Act was symptomatic of this attempt to reaffirm English culture and history as the norm. And draconian initiatives regarding asylum seekers and refugees, coupled with explicitly xenophobic speeches by prominent members of the government, serve to reinforce a political momentum which renders the even empathic multiculturalism of the 1970s hard to take for granted in the 1990s. At the level of the local state, specific funding for minority ethnic communities, such as existed with Section 11 funding, has now been absorbed into a generic Single Regeneration Fund, and the political will within local government to address racial inequality has in general significantly declined over the past decade.

It is perhaps therefore ironic that against this political context there has been a growing willingness of local authorities, employers and institutions to embrace *equal opportunity policies*. These policies are underpinned by a legal framework which incorporates gender, disability and sexual preference; and which therefore provides a broader constituency of self-interested parties who can accept at least the general principles involved. Additionally, equal opportunity policies explicitly stop short of positive discrimination. Consequently, while they may make explicit discrimination on racial grounds against individuals more difficult, their impact on patterns of inequality between different ethnic communities is very limited and slow (Jenkins and Solomos 1989). Equal opportunity policies are one means whereby multi-ethnic Britain comes to acknowledge the equal citizenship status of the great majority of their fellow residents. This is a reality which deserves to be noted.

The citizen and the nation in multi-ethnic Britain

The minority ethnic communities which have developed in Britain over the past five decades are predominantly constituted from peoples with long historical relationships with Britain. Coming initially from countries that were part of the British Empire, and which remain part of the Commonwealth, they arrived in Britain with a legal status that enabled them to be accepted as British citizens. Themselves, their children and their children's children are British citizens and enjoy a legal equivalence with the majority white population; all enjoy formal British citizenship. This is not a situation that can be assumed to apply in all Western European countries (Wrench and Solomos 1993). In Germany, for example, very substantial long-settled Turkish communities enjoy no such rights. For Britain, the significance of our shared citizenship has not always been fully understood by those discussing multi-ethnic policies. *Formal citizenship*, defined as 'membership in a nation state', should enable all citizens to enjoy equally a common *substantive citizenship*, defined as 'an array of civil, political, and especially social rights, involving also some kind of participation in the business of government' (Bottomore 1992). Where this is not the case, there are good reasons to enquire why some citizens should be privileged over others. And equally importantly, common citizenship rights should preclude any majority ethnic community from believing they are in a position to determine the rights of minority ethnic communities. Given common citizenship, members of minority ethnic communities expect equity in the services they receive as a matter of right, not as an extension of generosity by the majority community. This is not something the majority have always found easy to comprehend, or act upon.

The confusion has its roots in the political definition of the *nation*. As noted above, the idea of the British people has a very particular history and the recent concerted effort to define the British nation as being synonymous with English ethnicity necessarily marginalizes minority ethnic communities as an aberration within the imagined community (Anderson 1991) of the British nation. As long as the majority in Britain seek to define the nation in ethnocentric terms, the substantive rights of minority ethnic communities will always be jeopardized. Either their legitimate demands will be denied because they 'are not one of us', or their rights will be grudgingly granted and then claimed as an expression of the majority's tolerant generosity. This is no basis for developing equitable social policies within a *de facto* multi-ethnic nation.

Britain is a multi-ethnic society of predominantly fellow citizens, coexisting within a common state structure and sharing common institutions of education, law, welfare, health and social care. This is the common reality of all residents in Britain. What continue to differ widely are the political agendas which mobilize ethnicity and 'race' as variables which make problematic that diversity. And despite the near ubiquity of the rhetoric of equal opportunities, social policy in Britain is still informed by assimilationist, multicultural and anti-racist models for steering practice. All this is the context in which the nursing professions are now explicitly and seriously seeking to address the challenge of meeting the needs of an ethnically diverse client population.

Defining the user: the role of ethnicity

Ethnicity and identity

If the nursing professions are to respond to the challenge of ethnic diversity, they might usefully begin by clarifying what they understand *ethnicity* to be. As has been suggested above, one of the difficulties with the concept of ethnicity is that it seems alien to the majority ethnic communities' own experience. They are used to seeing it as a property of other people; something that *others* possess. For example, so much tourism is a nonsystematic exploration of the exotic other: a quick cultural smash and grab raid on conditions of engagement with the 'other' that have been determined well in advance. Thus ethnic dress, ethnic cuisine and ethnic values are routinely perceived as being vaguely exotic and different from the norm. It is *their difference* which makes it possible for the majority to see *them* as strange and exotic. Regrettably, members of the majority community do not take kindly to strangers who treat them as quaint and exotic. Similarly, many members of the majority white British society find that their route into making sense of the multi-ethnic society they inhabit starts from an unfortunately naive ethnocentrism: a natural seeming privileging of their own cultural values and practices as the norm. If the response to

Britain's multi-ethnic reality starts from such an ethnocentric recognition of difference, then it might reasonably be asked whether this is a meaningful improvement upon the 'colour blind', 'we treat everyone the same', conception of caring.

We are all ethnic, yet our ethnicity does not define us. We all need our ethnic identity to be respected, yet we cannot be adequately understood solely in terms of our ethnicity. What these statements point to is the complex nature of ethnicity and the variable implications it may have for our interaction with others.

Any attempt to treat ethnicity as a fixed property of individuals – ever present in shaping their behaviour and unchanging in its implications for how we should interact with them – is fatally flawed. At a social-psychological level ethnicity may be seen as being based in a 'consciousness of kind'. It is a form of self-categorization in which we know ourselves through our shared identity with other members of that ethnic category (Wallman 1986; see also Turner 1987). But we are all members of very many social categories; we have very many social identities. Importantly, however, not all these identities are actively in play at any one moment. From symbolic interactionist theorists to contemporary social constructionists there is a broad assertion of the malleability and complex flexibility of human identity (Burkitt 1991). They may invoke very different theoretical accounts of the phenomenon, but they support the common assertion of the plasticity of human identity. A complementary insight into the nature of human identity is consequently found in the assertion that ethnicity is *situational* (Wallman 1986). This means that ethnicity becomes relevant in particular contexts, in particular ways, in the presence of particular others. We are not like a stick of rock with our ethnicity permanently and continuously stamped throughout us.

Nor can it be assumed that when we find our ethnicity is relevant and actively expressed in our consciousness and behaviour, we are then in some sense like all other members of our ethnic group. This may occur to some extent in situations of extreme inter-ethnic conflict where inter-group dynamics generate strong in-group conformity (see, for example, Tajfel 1978; Turner 1987). Routinely, however, our behaviour reflects the complex dynamics of our identity. Not only, for example, do we have gender, class, age, ethnic, national and professional identities; we also learnt all of these in relation to each other, accommodating one to the other as we developed *our* competence in living these identities. Thus ethnicity is not a cultural micro-chip embedded identically into the identities of all members of a specific group. On the contrary, negotiating their ethnic identity is a competence all people have uniquely acquired as they cumulatively learned to incorporate and live their unique identities. Thus, for example, Black feminists have explored the complex dynamics of gender and ethnicity (hooks 1991; Mohanty *et al.* 1991; Bhavnani and Phoenix 1994); and contemporary human geographers have pointed out how differing experiences of migration, forced expulsion and historical dislocation may

place different individuals' conception of their ethnicity in a unique historically derived sense of time and space (Jackson and Penrose 1993; Keith
and Pile 1993).

What does all this imply for the nursing professions? At a minimal level
it requires an initial reflexive honesty of all practitioners as they make
explicit to themselves their own ethnicity. Following from this, it demands
the same intellectual and emotional openness as they interrogate their response to the reality of ethnic diversity among their client population.
Do they regard the values and practices of other ethnic communities in a
non-judgemental way as challengingly different, or as strange, or do they
see them as perverse and inferior? And it follows from the previous section that this will involve making explicit any implicit nationalist ethnocentrism which might result in their perceiving fellow citizens as being
treated favourably in being given the best professional care, 'despite their
ethnic minority status'. An ability to adopt a, perhaps self-conscious, cultural relativity is a necessary starting point for responding to ethnic diversity. Without that, the acquisition of knowledge about other communities
will be tainted at source, and minimal descriptive accuracy in bringing meaning and understanding to the behaviour of others will not be achievable.
This does not preclude value judgements, which may from a 'professional'
point of view be unavoidable, being at a later stage applied to this understanding. But surely it is a necessary prerequisite to professional caring
that we should understand clients, *on their own terms*, before we intervene
in their lives.

Regrettably, it follows from what has been said above that such understanding cannot be achieved through the rote learning of appropriate ethnic community information packs. There is the challenge of confronting
one's own ethnicity, as has just been noted, but there remains the further challenge of the complex nature of clients' experience of their own
ethnicity. There are very few 'simple rules of thumb', basic Health Service
Lonely Planet Guides to minority ethnic communities, which will furnish
an adequate basis for meeting the individual needs of particular clients.
The practitioner as tourist is not an attractive model for caring in a multi-
ethnic context. However, recognition of the real complexity of ethnicity
may be a further building block of appropriate care, and this is explored
further a few pages hence.

The infrastructural bases of ethnicity

Given the nursing profession's claims to practising holistic care, it is necessary that the client's ethnicity should be understood as involving more
than a sense of identity located in a shared culture. Ethnicity is more
than consciousness of kind, it also has structural characteristics (Wallman
1986). Ethnicity cannot survive and replicate itself only in people's minds;
their conscious sense of their ethnic identity must be capable of finding
expression in their behaviour and in shaping their material world. The

English in Britain can take their ethnicity almost for granted, for all the infrastructural resources are in place to allow them to express that identity, and to find it echoed back to them through the institutions which shape their experience. The English language can be spoken everywhere, there is no difficulty in eating English cuisine or in buying the basic ingredients for it, powerful images of their shared past are routinely present in the media and even in civic statuary. The system of law and the state educational system are consistent with the values and the traditions of English ethnicity. And 'English' modes of religious worship are privileged through the state religion and the wide availability of diverse places of Christian worship. In contrast, members of a small and recently arrived refugee community may find their religion regarded as alien, places of worship hard to locate, their preferred foodstuffs difficult to obtain, their language a barrier to social participation outside the home and small community, and their family kinship networks rendered unviable because of immigration regulations. Clearly, ethnicity cannot be adequately understood only as 'consciousness of kind'.

A holistic approach to ethnicity must locate specific ethnic identities within their own particular social, political, economic and material contexts. Persons with equally strong ethnic identities may differ widely in their access to control over resources that will enable that identity to be meaningfully lived in Britain. In relation to health care, this context will have very important consequences for individuals' perception of their health status, their health care needs and their ability to sustain models of health care practice that are consistent with their cultural conception of health and traditional means of remedying ill health.

Defining and negotiating the boundaries of ethnicity: implications for health care

The introduction of a structural element into our understanding of ethnicity opens up new insights and imposes new responsibilities upon the caring professions. If we started only from a social psychological conception of ethnicity as 'consciousness of kind' then we would certainly be capable of recognizing the fact that different ethnic communities have differing conceptions of health and illness. This would draw upon an understanding of identity rooted in *culture*; but it would be a perversely static view of culture. It would tend to be yet another variant upon the theme of ethnicity as something people possess. This time it is a 'culture' that *they* possess. And the logic of this form of conception of ethnicity is to seek to identify the cultural values and practices that are characteristic of this or that client's population. As we shall see below, a sensitive and flexible variation on this may well be appropriate. But cultures are not static and those elements within a culture which have particular significance in defining collective identities are not a permanent expression of some sort of historically determined essence. The anthropologist Frederik Barth (1969) criticized the definition of ethnicity in terms of artefacts and cultural practices: the 'ain't they quaint' fixation on the practices of isolated communities. He proposed that a more appropriate route into understanding ethnicity could be achieved through focusing upon how ethnic communities in contact with each other create and police the cultural boundaries between each other (Rex 1986). This approach instantly makes ethnic identity a dynamic and interactive phenomenon. We see that values and practices which become critical in defining ethnic identities serve two purposes: they are meaningful to members of the in-group and they are capable of identifying and excluding members of the out-group. Language is such a marker. It is a powerful resource of in-group identification and it subtly, or bluntly, identifies the incomer and the stranger. The English are not given to taking their medicines *per rectum*, and that might be sufficient to make them an alien, and difficult, patient in France. The point is that ethnic boundaries are socially created and routinely defined by a large number of ethnic markers. For those in the caring professions it is important to recognize that these boundaries are continuously negotiated in interaction, and consequently that minority ethnic communities in Britain are not independent of the majority populations, or the majority of the minority. Through interaction each contributes to defining the other.

The structural dimension of ethnicity reminds us that these interactions are not random. And for those in the caring professions it is important to recognize that the *institutions* in which they work have historically been vehicles of English ethnicity. This is a reality which is more likely to be evident to the minority ethnic user of health care than to the majority ethnic service provider. Additionally, a consciousness of the structural dimension of ethnicity may generate insight into the terms under which members of minority ethnic communities participate in state provision of care. The richness or paucity of infrastructural resources within a particular ethnic community may determine whether this participation is informed by a real choice. A small recently settled refugee community such as the Somali or Bosnian refugees may lack community resources which would provide a real alternative means of providing health care services. On the other hand, members of the Jewish community, or of some South Asian communities, may have available a range of complementary health care services. If a particular ethnic community does have access to a range of services which reflect its conception of health needs and provide culturally appropriate forms of care, this then opens up a further possibility; namely, that members of minority ethnic communities may, like the majority ethnic communities, exercise a flexible pattern of health care preferences (Sharma 1990; Ahmad 1992b). This may include using familiar community services to meet some needs and state provision for others. It may also include using both simultaneously (Smaje 1995). The variability of health care resources between different ethnic communities places a responsibility on health care providers to understand what these resources are. In the past, stereotypical conceptions of specific ethnic communities have resulted in naive and false assumptions being made about the availability of 'traditional' patterns of support. Inappropriate assumptions around the care of the Asian elderly are a case in point (Patel 1990; Blakemore and Boneham 1994). Equally, it is important that health care purchasers understand the range of health care resources available in particular communities in order to develop a care programme that makes realistic and optimum use of these ethnic community resources.

One aspect of the infrastructure of minority ethnic communities which has had a very significant impact upon the range of health care provision in Britain has been the growth of the Black and Asian voluntary sector in the past two decades or so. The very wide range of support to minority ethnic communities provided by these innovatory services has demonstrated how the health care needs of minority ethnic communities may be met with professional competence and ethnic sensitivity. Regrettably, a good deal of this provision has been generated out of resentment at the quality of treatment of members of minority ethnic communities within state provision. Perhaps mental health care has been the most visible of these responses, where state provision was found to be not only ethnically insensitive but also positively discriminatory (Fernando 1991; Sashidharan and Francis 1993). The growth of an ethnic minority voluntary and independent sector in health care provision is evidence of the strength and resilience of some minority ethnic communities. In the contemporary market context of health care delivery, there is a need for the statutory sector to learn how most effectively to mobilize these resources and benefit from their existence. At one level the voluntary sector is both a test-bed for good practice and a training resource for practitioners who may move over to mainstream provision. It is also a viable and valued means of providing appropriate care. Thus mainstream service purchasers need to learn how to incorporate the voluntary sector into their commissioning structures. More than that, given their control of major financial resources they need actively to participate in creating an extensive minority ethnic community independent sector, where agencies in the voluntary sector are able to cost their services realistically in order to survive and grow. Too often the commitment of the personnel in the voluntary sector of care provision is exploited and consequently their market value is undermined and their position within the health care services is marginalized.

The acceptance of *cultural pluralism*, as a diversity of cultural practices, within a multicultural response to ethnic diversity has very frequently masked a dominant community's resistance to *structural pluralism*, which offers the possibility of separate institutional structures. There has been fear and resentment that minority ethnic communities might achieve a degree of autonomy in their institutional resources; whether in education (for example, the resistance to Muslim schools), in politics (the resistance to Black sections) or in professional bodies (resistance to minority caucuses). Minority ethnic communities have a long experience of finding their attempts to attract appropriate resources for their community activities blocked and fragmented by the policies of state institutions (Anthias and Yuval-Davis 1993; Meekosha 1993). It is not in the interest of the health care services that this lamentable process should be allowed to continue to undermine the construction of a diverse, interactive and flexible multi-agency system of health care in Britain. Responding to ethnic diversity in Britain also requires a responsible recognition of the relevance and importance of the health care infrastructure within minority ethnic communities. Nor should this be seen as a policy designed only to benefit the members of minority ethnic communities. A flexible and efficient health service is of benefit to all. And what is now regarded as 'ethnic minority health provision' may reasonably be assumed to emerge at some future date as 'complementary medicine'; acupuncture being the most obvious current example.

Moving towards appropriate care

Conceptualizing the relation of self and other

The stranger undermines the spatial ordering of the world: the fought-after co-ordination between moral and topographical closeness, the staying together of friends and the remoteness of enemies. The stranger disturbs the resonance between physical and psychical distance – he [sic] is physically near while remaining spiritually remote. He brings into the inner circle of proximity the kind of difference and otherness that are anticipated and tolerated at a distance – where they can be dismissed as irrelevant or repelled as inimical. The stranger represents an incongruous and hence resented 'synthesis of nearness and remoteness'.

(Bauman 1990: 150)

This idea of the 'stranger' as neither friend nor enemy, as someone physically among us and yet emotionally not one of us, is a useful analogy for the cross-cultural encounter in the context of providing nursing care. Because of the nature of the recent history of the arrival and settlement of minority ethnic communities in Britain, people of differing ethnic identities came to be located in particular conurbations (Rose 1969), and predominantly housed within particular parts of these cities. There has been an extensive physical separation of minority ethnic communities from the majority ethnic population. Additionally, as we have already seen above, these 'immigrants' came with attached stereotypes of inferiority and difference, which became amplified through the growth of a racist reaction to their settlement in Britain. Thus it is not unreasonable to talk of the majority ethnic service providers and the minority ethnic service users as in many ways being strangers to each other. From the majority perspective *they* are not of *us*, but they are among us. The consequence of this state of affairs is routinely anxiety: a fear of the uncertainty of what may be expected, of how communication may break down and of the violation of *our* routine. The fact of a stranger being a member of a once immigrant, now settled, minority ethnic community population has the added possibility that their presence here is resented as illegitimate: 'they should not be here to threaten our life style'. The English ethno-nationalism, discussed above, may add an undercurrent of moral outrage to the uncertainty and anxiety of encounters with the 'stranger'. Strategies of segregation, as, for example, in housing, which reduce the probability of encounters, or of rejection, as in a racist refusal to acknowledge someone as present in your company, are not permissible options for practitioners in the nursing professions. In a multi-ethnic society all practitioners must transcend any propensity to retreat from recognizing and responding to the ethnic diversity present among their client population. Invoking a humanistic assertion that we are all the same, and we treat everyone the same, also will not do. The reality of difference must be recognized as legitimate; and that difference must be negotiated through interaction.

Bauman's (1990) discussion of responses to 'the stranger' is interestingly echoed in the literature on cross-cultural communication, where the ambiguity surrounding appropriate behaviour stems from an unfamiliarity with the other's culture. This ambiguity then generates anxiety and a lack of confidence in anticipating appropriate rules for interaction (Lalljee 1987; Gudykunst 1988). Where this anxiety develops in an interaction between members of different ethnic groups it is probable that group identities may be invoked stereotypically as a means of reducing uncertainty. By labelling the other we reduce his or her unique individuality to the characteristics of the group; but that does have the short-term benefit of introducing a false sense of certainty into the consequent interaction. Not only does this process confirm our certainty about who *they* are, it simultaneously makes relevant our identity and consequently through self-stereotyping gives certainty about who we are (Turner and Giles 1981; Turner 1987; Kim 1989). The introduction of such 'intergroup postures' into cross-cultural interaction inevitably creates distortion and is likely to produce a feedback loop of inappropriate perception, insensitive behaviour and mutual resentment, which feeds upon itself in a spiral of frustration and recrimination.

An ability to negotiate unfamiliar environments often includes a degree of 'culture shock' (Furnham and Bochner 1986) and in cross-cultural nursing and midwifery contacts this constitutes a challenge for both the client and the carer. This is a stressful experience for both. As one authority on intercultural communication has said,

The above intercultural challenges – cultural difference and intergroup posture – lead to stress. Stress experiences, no matter how minimal, are inherent in the very nature of the intercultural communication context ... Stress, indeed, is considered part and parcel of intercultural encounters, disturbing the internal equilibrium of the individual system.

Accordingly, to be interculturally competent means to be able to manage such stress, regain the internal balance, and carry out the communication process in such a way that contributes to successful interaction outcomes.

(Kim 1992: 376)

Conceptualizing competence in cross-cultural contexts

It is certainly appropriate to expect both partners in such a stressful cross-cultural encounter to work at overcoming the difficulties it may present. However, in the context of the nursing professions it is clear that at least one of the partners is under an obligation to seek to overcome the stress and difficulties involved. Members of the nursing professions, as professionals, are required to ensure that they meet the health care needs of all of their clients. Racist strategies of retreat or rejection are ethically unacceptable; and they may well violate the law against racial discrimination. At a less extreme level, the routine anxiety experienced in cross-cultural contexts can be legitimately acknowledged within the caring context. Indeed, it must be acknowledged and addressed. The time has come for the nursing professions to embrace competence in managing cross-cultural interaction as being as much a part of their professional competencies as aseptic techniques or the administration of drugs.

Fortunately, there is abundant evidence that we can all learn to manage cross-cultural encounters with some sensitivity and efficiency (Furnham and Bochner 1986; Kareem and Littlewood 1992). We can examine this process of learning to manage cross-cultural interaction by identifying two possible ways of defining what it is that is to be learnt. Kim (1992) distinguishes between culture-specific communicative competence and intercultural communicative competence. We suggest later that we call these competencies in simultaneous interaction *transcultural communicative competence*.

As these terms imply, *cultural communicative competence* requires the individual to learn to understand the cultural values, behavioural patterns and rules for interaction in specific cultures. This draws very heavily on anthropological insights into specific cultures and provides an understanding of both the rules of politeness governing interaction and the very specific behavioural actions that carry particular meaning for members of that culture. Thus rules governing how close you should stand together when talking or whether you should touch each other while interacting may differ widely from one culture to another (Hall 1959, 1966; Argyle 1975). Getting this wrong can severely disrupt the interaction; since what in one culture may be a physical interaction that signifies continuing polite interest in what you are saying, in another may be a claim to considerable personal intimacy. Even those almost unconscious gestures which we incorporate into our everyday speech may be far from innocent, since they can have very different meanings in different cultures (Morris 1979). These variations in what constitutes the 'normal' patterning of behaviour while interacting with others from a different culture can be identified and taught, employing the same forms of social skills training that might be involved in remedying social skills deficits within a culture (Hollin and Trower 1986).

Thus at one level acquiring cultural communicative competence involves learning how to manage your behaviour so as to put those to whom you are speaking at ease, and create an environment in which you can then efficiently exchange the meanings, ideas, information and issues which are essential to professional care (see, for example, Danziger (1976) on the distinction between representation and presentation in interaction situations). However, for efficient and appropriate care, members of the nursing professions need to know not only how to interact in terms of managing their own behaviour; they also need to understand the values and cultural prescriptions operating within the client's culture, particularly those which may impinge upon the client's conception of health and illness, and their expectations around bodily functions. Those inevitable aspects of the human condition, such as birth and death, eating and defecating, are in every society overlaid with a rich cultural text of prescriptions and proscriptions, rituals and values. We consequently need to be able to anticipate what dietary requirements a particular culture *may* impose upon a client, or how death must be managed, or how the client's sense of cleanliness and pollution may have significance for the preparation and serving of meals, or the washing of clothing and bodies. To be culturally communicatively competent we require knowledge of the values and expectations that are the cultural element of an individual's ethnicity. This information is not generalizable to an encounter with 'strangers' from other communities, it is culture specific. Thus, in a multi-ethnic society, to be culturally communicatively competent in relation to a number of different ethnic communities does constitute a significant challenge to the caring professions.

However, in proposing the concept of *intercultural communicative competence*, Kim (1992) is suggesting that there may be generic communicative skills which at least prepare us to be optimally flexible and adept at meeting the challenge of intercultural interactions; regardless of the specific cultures involved in the exchange. He starts by referring back to the stress that is inherent in cross-cultural interaction, and proposes that it is the possession of a range of abilities which enables the individual to handle and transcend that stress which is at the core of intercultural communicative competence. 'In other words, individuals who hope to carry out effective intercultural interactions must be equipped with a set of abilities to be able to understand and deal with the dynamics of cultural difference, intergroup posture, and the inevitable stress experience' (Kim 1992: 376).

Not surprisingly, therefore, Kim identifies adaptability as being at the heart of this competence. It is a capacity to suspend or modify your own cultural expectations and to be able to accommodate to new cultural demands. It is an ability to respond flexibly and creatively to the challenges of cultural difference and intergroup posture, and to manage the stress generated by these in ways that do not distort your ability to respond to 'the stranger'. This really means that such an individual has learnt to transcend defensive responses to difference and has avoided rigid mental and behavioural strategies for handling the stress of cross-cultural interaction.

Kim suggests that we may reasonably expect this adaptability to be expressed in three different dimensions of human behaviour; the cognitive, the affective and the behavioural dimension.

In the area of cognition, Kim invokes the literature on cognitive styles, in which cognitive simplicity – having a limited repertoire of concepts – is compared with cognitive complexity (Applegate and Sypher 1988); or cognitive rigidity is opposed to cognitive flexibility (Kim 1989). The *cognitive dimension* of intercultural competence is therefore a creative flexibility in one's thought processes. It is a refusal to be dogmatic, or to insist on reducing new experiences to familiar and safe categories of understanding.

The *affective dimension* is an emotional and aesthetic complement to this cognitive style. It is defined by the absence of ethnocentrism (Brewer and Campbell 1976) and prejudice (Allport 1954; Husband 1994). On the positive side, it is characterized by empathy (Ruben and Kealey 1979) and a willingness to be emotionally positive and open to the other. The affective dimension thus refers to how we have learnt to negotiate our feelings, whether through an inner-directed, protective, setting of boundaries to our emotional identification with others, or through a positive and other-directed emotional openness in our encounter with others. The former renders every intercultural encounter an emotional threat, while the latter makes it an opportunity for growth.

The *behavioural dimension* relates to our ability to express in our actions those insights and feelings that are generated by the previous two dimensions. We may know what is expected in a situation and wish to participate appropriately but find ourselves awkward and inhibited in following this through into behaviour. In our own culture we may feel that in relation to joining in dancing, or singing in front of friends, or 'letting our hair down' in a way that is not familiar to us. In ethnology, the study of animal behaviour, the concept of 'behavioural repertoire' has proved to be useful. This refers to the range of behaviours available to the animal as part of its experience. The wider our behavioural repertoire, the more flexibility we may expect to have in adapting to new situations. If you are used to eating tripe you may find it less challenging than some to eat sushi; or if you are used to 'dressing up for the occasion' in Britain you may find it easier to adopt the appropriate dress codes when operating within other cultural contexts. Like the dimensions before it, the behavioural dimension is all about our ability to adapt and be flexible in new situations.

Intercultural communicative competence is, then, an invitation to examine our capacity to acquire generic skills which will enable us to enter into any intercultural context with a degree of confidence about our ability to cope. It is a confidence based on an experience of being adaptable. It is a confidence founded on our knowing that we can rapidly learn what is required to ensure efficient and appropriate interaction; unlike in cultural communicative competence, where the confidence resides in already knowing about *this* culture. Clearly one type of competence feeds off the other. In Kim's words,

> intercultural communicative competence and cultural communicative competence must be clearly distinguished as separate conceptual domains, even though both operate together in any given intercultural encounter. While the content of cultural communicative competence clearly varies from culture to culture, the content of intercultural communicative competence should remain constant across all intercultural situations regardless of specific cultures involved.
>
> (Kim 1992: 373)

We suggest that in order to retain conceptual clarity, the term *transcultural communicative competence* be used to refer to both forms of competence operating as a creative, synchronized, cross-cultural interaction. Thus transcultural communicative competence is an integrated performance drawing appropriately upon elements of intercultural and cultural competence. Clearly, in relation to the nursing professions both forms of competence must be developed. The generic adaptability of intercultural communicative competence is a means of preparing the practitioner to be open and flexible in response to any cross-cultural interaction. It involves the acquisition of a cognitive style and an attitudinal stance towards 'the stranger' which prevents the practitioner from artificially and hastily reducing the ambiguity present in the encounter. It enables the practitioner to work with that ambiguity through an open and empathetic negotiation of the client's identity and needs. This competence must surely exist as a necessary range of abilities characteristic of any practitioner who claims to offer holistic care. To engage with the client in his or her entirety must presume a competence in sustaining an open and non-egocentric continuous dialogue with him or her.

At the same time, in any specific cross-cultural interaction there is also present the requirement for the practitioner to familiarize himself or herself with the specific implications for practice of the client's culture and identity. This cultural communicative competence must be uniquely developed in relation to each distinct ethnic identity. And as we have seen above, ethnicity is complex. The contemporary debates around the complexity and hybridity of ethnic identities, linked with the past critiques of the use of ethnicity, might reasonably make any practitioner nervous in addressing the relevance of ethnicity for meeting the needs of clients. In our research we have found an awareness among nurses of the dangerous possibility of stereotyping clients by assuming that they possess the characteristics associated with their ethnic group. This is a dilemma; for without the essential knowledge base of cultural communicative competence we cannot begin to anticipate what particular beliefs *may* shape a client's perception of illness, what cultural prescriptions we should be alerted to and consequently what rituals or cultural practices *may* have relevance for the process of caring. Without this framework of specific knowledge, the practitioner cannot begin the unique interpersonal negotiation with clients over what if any of these possibilities may be relevant to them. Prior knowledge of *what might be relevant* allows the practitioner to develop the appropriate repertoire of behavioural skills, from which those appropriate to the specific client may be selected. And, of course, the ability to operate at such a sophisticated level will necessarily draw upon the generic skills of intercultural communicative competence.

Acknowledging competence and transcending the fear of failure

The possibility of things going wrong, of being seen to get it wrong, is always present in any cross-cultural interaction. Under any circumstances this is awkward and embarrassing. In a professional context this may be experienced as threatening to one's personal confidence and professional standing. As we shall see in subsequent chapters, the nursing professions to date have in general been inadequately prepared to meet the challenge of cross-cultural practice through their professional training. Yet as we have already noted, the nursing professions are under increasing pressure, and scrutiny, to demonstrate a professional competence in meeting the needs of all clients. Being required to carry out duties for which you know yourself to be ill-equipped is a distressing activity, and one often handled through short-term defensive strategies which ultimately aggravate the situation. This situation may usefully be placed within Howell's (1982) model of competence.

First, there is (a) *unconscious incompetence*, where we misinterpret other's behaviour and respond inappropriately. This is a state of grace, for at this point we proceed with our routine oblivious of our contribution to the distress we cause others.

Then we may learn the error of our ways and we enter into (b) *conscious incompetence*, where we are painfully aware of our incompetence but feel unable to do very much about it. That is the most painful transition in any professional learning experience. To be moved from ignorant, comfortable incompetence to the perpetual itch of self-conscious incompetence can be terribly threatening. It can produce a catastrophic loss of confidence that produces a panic response when you must enter into the situation of your known inadequacy. In the caring professions this has been seen to produce a 'freezing' of majority ethnic staff when placed in a multi-ethnic working context. When any action may be 'wrong', one response is to do nothing; and this may involve not even employing the skills you do possess. This response is a form of personal disempowerment in which the challenge is declared to be too great, and a series of avoidance strategies are invoked in order to retreat from addressing an area of known incompetence. For any individual this is regrettable and stressful.

When this becomes a shared strategy of a work team, or an institution, it is disastrous for professional–client relations. However, such freezing may be avoided, or with effort reversed, through a deliberate willingness to address the deficit, and systematically to seek to acquire the necessary skills.

This then leads to (c) *conscious competence*, where we continue to be self-conscious about our interaction, but it is experienced as a positive process of developing competence. In terms of intercultural communicative competence, this stage may involve a letting go of acquired mental and emotional strategies that have created a defensive rigidity in your response to others. It may be a period of experimenting with new ideas, of allowing new experiences to happen and of responding to them with a curiosity that allows for a positive emotional engagement. In terms of cultural communicative competence, it would be a period of focused learning, as relevant facts are absorbed and new ways of behaving are incorporated into your repertoire. All of this includes the possibility of making mistakes. However, with the appropriate learning environment, and with the appropriate support, these should be experienced as key opportunities for learning and the honing of skills.

It is possible that in a world of multi-ethnic complexity and continuing social change members of the nursing profession should anticipate that conscious competence may remain an ever present element in their cross-cultural interactions as a practitioner. However, there is in Howell's model a final stage that may be attainable.

(d) *Unconscious competence* is achieved when a practitioner has acquired the skills for communication and efficient interaction to the extent that he or she is now spontaneous and no longer needs to be consciously monitored. At this stage the personal cognitive, affective and behavioural skills of intercultural communicative competence would have become an integrated system enabling the practitioner to be flexible and adaptive. In relation to specific minority ethnic communities, there would be an extensive familiarity with their culture and a proficiency in identifying what elements of it may be relevant to any particular client.

Conclusion

It is apparent that the challenge to the nursing professions presented by the *de facto* multi-ethnic nature of contemporary Britain is one which impacts upon individual practitioners, those responsible for nursing and midwifery education and those responsible for the development and oversight of the professions; as well as upon those service providers who employ practitioners, and those who purchase these services. While the research reported here demonstrates that nursing and midwifery education has barely begun to address this challenge systematically, it must also be noted that there is a range of extant literature which addresses the question of transcultural nursing, and which offers frameworks for professional development. These include North American contributions such as Leininger (1978) and Block and Monroy (1983) and British contributions such as Mares *et al.* (1985) and Dobson (1992). However, there is inadequate information regarding the variety of ways in which the insights from authors such as these are incorporated into education and practice. And as we indicate below in the research findings, there is evidence of an *ad hoc* and minimalist response to preparing practitioners to meet the needs of a multi-ethnic clientele in English nursing and midwifery education. The discussion of ethnicity sketched above should serve as a warning against any assumption that developing intercultural competence and ethnic sensitivity in individual practitioners will of itself constitute a sufficient response. Transculturally competent practitioners are not in themselves sufficient to guarantee an equitable health care system.

As noted above, it is essential to examine those systematic structures of power over resources within institutions which determine both the type of resources made available, and their distribution across client populations. The hierarchy of needs which is evident within service provision is not a simple reflection of the distribution of needs across the client populations. For example, illnesses, like sickle-cell and thalassaemia, which disproportionately impact upon significant proportions of minority ethnic communities have historically been neglected in research and treatment priorities, with other illnesses impacting upon a smaller proportion of the majority population being given a greater priority. At another level, the demographic location of minority ethnic communities in inner-city areas may result in their particular needs having to be met within health care contexts which are generically underresourced. Any number of competent transcultural practitioners are not likely to impact upon the political process which allows inequalities of provision between health authorities to persist. And as was suggested above, the users' preference for particular forms of, and contexts for, treatment may mean that health authority initiatives in prioritizing improved access to existing resources for minority ethnic communities may be inappropriate. Some users might prefer equally cost-effective services within the minority independent sector to be made available.

Thus, the production of transculturally competent practitioners is a necessary task in the context of contemporary British health care. Ensuring an effective and sensitive mode of interpersonal communication in practitioner–client interaction is rewarding for both participants; as well as being a professional necessity in ensuring good nursing and midwifery care. But it cannot be the practitioners alone who must demonstrate creative adaptability; the health care system must show an ability to respond flexibly to the health care needs of minority ethnic service users.

3

Messages from the users: minority ethnic users' experience of nursing care

Introduction

The message contained in Chapter 2 is intended to convey the unequivocal complexity of ethnicity as a phenomenon in contemporary society, and the absolute necessity of locating current attempts of social policy to respond to ethnic diversity into a critical historical perspective. Only from such a starting point will it be possible to adopt an appropriate degree of sophistication and caution in beginning to address the users' experience of health care provision in general, and nursing and midwifery care in particular. An understanding of the demography and structural location of minority ethnic communities in Britain will itself promote an understanding of the genesis of the health care needs of minority communities. The history of migration and settlement of each minority ethnic community provides a background to their current demography. For many, this includes a disproportionate location within the inner-city areas of large metropolitan districts, and a class profile distinctly skewed downwards (Skellington 1992). Indeed, in discussing Britain's minority ethnic communities, sociologists of differing theoretical persuasion have spoken of the way in which 'race' has distorted the location of such minorities within the British class system, to the extent that they constitute a marginalized class fraction (Phizacklea and Miles 1980) or underclass (Rex and Tomlinson 1979). Thus a necessary basis for understanding the health care needs of minority communities resides in an understanding of the consequences of their class profile. A major determinant of an individual's health and social care needs, and of the likelihood of these needs being met, is his or her position within the class system (Townsend and Davidson 1982; Whitehead 1987; DoH 1995b). Consequently, many of the processes which determine the health care needs of specific minority ethnic communities reflect the environmental and lifestyle consequences of their class position. In this sense, minority ethnic communities' health care needs, and their experience of how they are met, are a consequence of these structural features of British society which they share with others in the same class. It follows, therefore, that an analysis of minority ethnic communities' health care needs and provision as solely explicable in terms of *their* ethnicity is inadequate and inaccurate. An ethnic definition of need necessarily obscures the social and structural basis of the need, and helps to perpetuate the marginalization of the minority client (Ahmad and Husband 1993). A fixation with the 'race' of clients and with attempting to account for their health care needs in terms of their culture is naively reductionist, and has been robustly criticized as a racialization of the minority ethnic community's experience (Ahmad 1993b).

> Racialization assumes that 'race' is the primary, natural and neutral means of categorisation, and that the groups are distinct also in behaviour characteristics, which result from their 'race' . . .
>
> Racialization takes place in terms of notions of cultures being static and homogeneous and having a biological basis. This is then extended to notions of cultures having direct relationship to attitudes, expectations and behaviour. 'Cultures' here take on a rigid and constraining shape, rather than being nurturing and sustaining forces. These culturalist assumptions ignore issues of power, deprivation and racism. They result in culturalist explanations and feed into culturalist health policy options.
>
> (Ahmad 1993b: 18–19)

Almost perversely, having just echoed such a forthright warning against the error of racialization, we need to make the seemingly contradictory assertion that the health care needs of minority ethnic communities must be understood in relation to their distinct cultural values and practices. This is the essence of cross-cultural care discussed above. The resolution of this apparent contradiction lies in noting that it is the insertion of a sensitive cultural awareness into a structural analysis of the health status of minority ethnic communities that is required. Neither an exclusively culturalist nor an exclusively structural analysis of health care needs can be acceptable. Processes of racist exclusion and of class interact complexly (Rex and Mason 1986).

In a range of ways the discriminatory processes of racism have shaped the class profile of minority ethnic communities, and continue to exacerbate the negative consequences of their class position: they suffer a double jeopardy. Additionally, the experience of being a member of a marginalized minority ethnic community, subject to racist assault, insult and subtle discrimination, impacts very significantly upon minority communities' conscious understanding of their life in Britain. Yet while majority racism may make 'race' an issue in their lives, it is through the resources of their shared ethnic identity that minority ethnic communities seek to resist and challenge such discrimination. For such minority communities racism is part of their external environment, while ethnicity is part of their lived identity. Thus, in discussing minority ethnic clients' experience of nursing and midwifery care, they may express racism as one of the determining factors in their ill-health; and also explain their distinctive, ethnic-based, understanding of what constitutes ill-health and how it may be appropriately treated.

The health status of minority ethnic communities has received increasing attention, with general measures of mortality (Marmot *et al.* 1984; Balarajan and Bulusu 1990) and morbidity rates (Benezeval *et al.* 1992) being complemented by analyses of the prevalence of specific diseases among particular ethnic communities (Balarajan and Raleigh 1993). More recently, an inclusive overview of the health care needs of minority ethnic communities has been provided by Smaje (1995), and a recent NHS funded review of research based evidence on ethnicity and health complements Smaje's text (Centre for Reviews and Dissemination 1996). There is therefore a growing body of literature which makes possible a research-informed evaluation of the health care needs of minority ethnic clients. Differential morbidity rates may require a sensitive definition of priorities in planning health resources, and the provision of appropriate diagnostic screening of populations at particular risk.

However, epidemiological data provide but one necessary element in the planning of health care services. The clients' own understanding of their health status must also be addressed; for Western medicine offers only one of a range of ways in which we human beings have come to conceptualize good health and its counterpart, illness. Medical diagnostic categories may provide a very poor fit to clients' own understanding of their health care needs and how they might be appropriately addressed. Here again, Smaje (1995) provides a brief insight into the range of health beliefs which may be expected among minority ethnic communities in Britain. This review indicates the ways in which ideas from Western and non-Western models of health may be employed by minority ethnic clients. The provision of appropriate care therefore places a responsibility upon the practitioner to incorporate this possibility into the interaction with the client. Given the ubiquitous claim to offer holistic care, which is evident among the nursing professions, this is a charge on nurses' and midwives' professional competence which should be compatible with their own self-image.

The user's perspective

The types of data collected and their appropriate use

While an intellectual understanding of non-Western philosophies of health may be acquired through reading appropriate texts (for example, Said 1983; Williams 1995) and through formal instruction, this provides an arid unlived account of how meaning is brought to someone's experience of their health. Thus a necessary supplement to such intellectual understanding is a biographical account of health care users' experience of their health care. There exists a body of research literature on minority ethnic users' experience of health care (for example, Judge and Solomon 1993; Pilgrim *et al.* 1993) which suggests that both ethnic identity and racism may be elements in shaping their experience. This literature is additionally complemented by more discursive accounts of minority ethnic communities' experience of health care (for example, Bryan *et al.* 1985; Wilson 1994). The user's voice is an important, and irreplaceable, source of expertise. Users know how their culture has relevance for their conception of good health and appropriate care. They, as the recipients of health care services, can identify the ways in which racism and cultural ignorance impinge upon service delivery. They have unique insights into how nursing care may be improved. While the Department of Health has recognized the importance of the users' perspectives in its various initiatives and research strategy, they are as yet a largely untapped resource in shaping health care services and in informing nursing and midwifery education. However, it is in recognition of the fact that health authorities and health trusts are beginning to seek to tap this users' expertise that we have deliberately, in this chapter, used the concept of user rather than client. The 'user's voice', the 'user's experience', the 'user's panel' are increasingly a part of the discourse of health service planning and management; and this is a policy trend we would wish to support.

As a modest contribution to persuading nursing professionals to tap the rich experience of the users, we have within this project sought to complement the extant published literature with qualitative data derived from minority ethnic communities. We have carried out 75 interviews which have accessed the view of Afro-Caribbean, Chinese, Gujarati, Irish, Jewish, Pakistani, Polish, Sikh and Somali users of nursing and midwifery care. These interviews, where appropriate, have been carried out in the community language of the users. Given the limited resources available for this activity, the interviews can in no way be regarded as a social scientifically adequate sampling of the range of experiences within the communities contacted. No attempt was made to 'sample' the communities identified above, since this would have required a very considerable increase in the number of interviews to be carried out. Rather, existing contacts with researchers and professionals from the minority communities were employed to identify community organizations and individuals who could facilitate access to interviews. The accent was upon obtaining spontaneous, open responses from those interviewed. These interviews are indicative of the range of experience of care found among a diverse range of minority ethnic users. They cannot be added together as a social scientific sample, but they do offer snapshots of individual experiences which cannot be lightly dismissed.

The interviews have provided the research team with first-hand experience of the opinions represented elsewhere at second-hand, in the more neutral tones of research reports such as those cited above. They have provided a source of direct experience of nursing and midwifery care. There are negative experiences to be found recurrently in these data; some of them shocking. There is also evidence of user satisfaction, and of a sympathetic understanding of the circumstances in which practitioners seek to provide good care.

It should be noted that our interviewers, in gaining access for the data, encountered varying degrees of resistance and scepticism about health-related research. Some of the people contacted explicitly expressed scepticism about the value of participating in research such as this given their experience of the apparent irrelevance for practice of previous research. This sentiment was encountered much more robustly by one of the researchers who attempted to invite minority ethnic voluntary groups to prepare formal position statements which reflected their members' experience of nursing and midwifery care. While some such statements were forthcoming, the prolonged negotiation necessitated in eliciting others resulted in this form of data collection being abandoned within the time constraints of the project. That the researcher requesting this information was from a majority ethnic group was very probably a factor. But the strength of the pre-existing views among members of minority ethnic communities about the irrelevance of past research to changing their experience of health and social care was itself a potent and unambiguous phenomenon. To some, research was seen as a self-serving activity which had little credibility for minority community activists. Past research was seen as being informed by the concerns of the majority and exploited in the interests of the same majority community. Many of the individual interviewees echoed something of this anxiety in preferring not to have their interviews tape-recorded.

So in the following pages the reader may wish to reflect upon the generosity of spirit of the interviewees who gave their time and shared their experiences; possibly despite an inclination to feel that yet again they might be being misrepresented or exploited. We have deliberately attempted to convey something of the users' experience through a heavy reliance upon their own words. If we are unable to assert that these experiences are a representative sample of minority ethnic communities' experiences, we may yet remind the reader that they are reflections of users' unique individual experience. Some of these experiences invite the response: this should not be capable of happening; ever. Others challenge all members of the nursing professions to enquire how they may benefit from them by seeking to modify their own practice.

Language as an issue in service delivery

A recurrent issue emerging in the data from the users' interviews was the importance of language as a factor in their experience of nursing and midwifery care. An inability to share a common language obviously presents a major obstacle to understanding; either in the description of symptoms or in comprehending the treatment that is being offered. But there are many aspects of communication that are problematic beyond the absolute incomprehension of linguistic exclusion. A link is made between communication and respect in a comment within a statement from an organization which serves a very large number of Gujarati women:

> As has already been indicated language barriers can result in feelings of exclusion; of women not being part of the discussion about their own health needs or care. The reliance on children to translate is neither adequate or advisable and although there is an interpretation service at the hospitals it does not seem to be adequate for their needs. Even where women spoke good or reasonable English they encountered problems in getting their questions answered.
>
> In addition, attitudes which are dismissive or patronising can block communication from day one. It only takes one rough comment from one doctor or nurse to promote the perception that that is how things are generally. When you are vulnerable by virtue of being ill and prostrate in front of someone in a uniform it is extraordinarily difficult to have a discussion as an equal unless every effort is made to assist this to happen. If you already know that your place in British society is considered to be on the lower rungs this adds to the feeling of vulnerability. Many women also said that they did not know where to complain or to whom but even if they did they would feel very frightened about doing so in case it had an adverse affect on their treatment.
>
> To respect someone as an equal must be a condition of good nursing care and this involves examining the racism and sexism involved so often in the treatment of Asian women.

This statement introduces a much more complex perspective on the communicative context, in which language is but one of the more obvious agendas. Where there is no common language a translation service is an obvious, and necessary, resource. Too often users speak of using children, relatives or friends to act as translators, an experience also reported by others (Ahmad and Walker 1996). This introduces a whole range of limitations into the interaction between service provider and service user. There is no reason to believe that the *ad hoc* 'translator' has adequate linguistic competence to achieve this task efficiently. Specifically, they may be ill informed or ignorant of the medical jargon employed by the health professional and hence resort to guessing or merely having to declare that they have no idea of what is being said. Additionally, there is the very real problem of confidentiality where both symptoms and treatment may be painfully awkward to share with a friend or family member. Thus the absence of an adequate interpretation service may lead to distressing or inefficient health care experiences, or to users failing to keep appointments: experiences which were echoed in the users' data (Shackman 1985). There is also some evidence to suggest that these factors influence clients' choice of practitioner and limit their access to appropriate health care (Ahmad *et al.* 1989).

Nor can it be assumed that linguistic boundaries are explicit or unambiguous. As the statement from an African-Caribbean support group indicates, the language varieties employed within their communities constitute a particular challenge to the nursing professions:

> There is an ongoing debate about whether African-Caribbean people speak a different language or whether it is 'broken English'. We certainly would not say that it is broken English as this implies that it is somehow less than a proper way of speaking. Patois and Creole are definitely languages in themselves and variations of these abound. For some African people English therefore is not their first language; but whereas this is more recognised for Asian communities, African-Caribbean people are viewed as if they are just not making enough effort, or speaking that way to be awkward. Whatever the debate it is vital that assumptions are not made about understanding.

The variety of ways in which language may impact upon a client's experience of care may be suggested by a brief listing of some examples.

- A Chinese client admitted to hospital with a suspected heart attack reported that on the first day the treatment was good but by the second day she felt that she was being ignored, as she couldn't communicate with the nurses. If her family had not translated and completed the menu for her, she felt that she wouldn't have eaten anything. (L.C.3)
- Another Chinese client, having been admitted to hospital for surgery, was not mobile following the operation. She reported that during the night she was not asked if she required the toilet and neither was a bedpan provided. She described this as 'an utterly humiliating experience and all because I was unable to communicate effectively in English. Why should the effort always be up to us to make?' (L.C.6)
- A Somali woman spoke of her experience of care, in which language was her only problem, and she felt a need for nursing professionals who spoke her language: 'An interpreter or sometimes a friend can interpret for you. If a nurse tells you something, like deep inside you – your uterus – things inside, maybe the midwife, if it is a midwife, can explain to you because she knows everything; she knows maybe in Somali the proper word for that. Maybe an interpreter, or the friend doesn't know the real word for it. She will tell, but she won't explain as a Somali midwife could.' (A.8.1)
- A Gujarati Hindu woman reported that, 'Last week I took my mum's friend down to the hospital, she was 61. She had a note from the doctor to say – bring an interpreter with you, as there is no one on the ward that can interpret for you.' After admission language remained a problem, since 'she found out later that when it came to food the nurses would just tick the choices for her, as she could not read or understand English. The nurses had been told that she was a vegetarian, but the variations of interpretation of this can be broad . . . So in effect she had no choice of what she ate.' (G.8)

The provision of skilled translators is much appreciated, as this statement from an 'Asian carers group' exemplifies:

It is not that we expect all staff to speak all languages, but to have a few more people around with more translators would help. Recently though [over the past two years] one of our members has noticed that he has been asked on making an appointment for his mother whether she needed an interpreter. This we see as a really good way of doing things. That is instead of making assumptions or guessing or struggling, people are asked about their needs and then there is a service available to meet them.

Respect and the recognition of difference: the attitudinal dimension

As the statement from the Gujarati women's organization points out, there is much more to effective communication than mere linguistic skill. The relative status of the participants, and the attitudes expressed by one towards the other, have a major impact upon what is shared and exchanged. Intonation and body posture may say very much more than a health care service provider may wish to acknowledge. Explicit verbal insults and racial epithets are not necessary to convey to a client a practitioner's sense of hostility and resentment: 'intergroup posture' may be more than adequately declared through non-verbal communication (Roberts *et al.* 1992). Thus linguistic competence alone is not a sufficient criterion for evaluating the quality of cross-cultural communication. An ability to demonstrate respect for the client and a degree of understanding of his or her world view are equally essential. Negative attitudes and cultural ignorance recur within the users' comments as a significant disruptive force within the carer–client relationship. This is illustrated in a statement from an Afro-Caribbean mental health project:

Nurses play a very important role in the front line delivery of mental health care to Afro-Caribbean people, work that often goes unrecognised. However, they undoubtedly play a part in the negative experience that Black people have in hospital. Perceptions and attitudes of white people towards Black people influence their treatment in hospital. These perceptions and attitudes are often based on a lack of knowledge and understanding about Black people.

It is perhaps not surprising that negative attitudes and cross-cultural ignorance should be associated. For practitioners with racist sentiments there is no incentive to understand anything of a minority ethnic community's culture, save only to sustain those stereotypical beliefs which confirm their hostility. For practitioners who are ignorant of clients' cultures it may be that their anxiety and awkwardness makes their communicative style formal and stilted, and open to interpretation as being negative or hostile. 'Group posture' is not a monopoly of the majority community, and the recurrent encounters of members of minority ethnic communities with racism and marginalization within British society may have made them highly sensitive to the nuances of interpersonal communication across ethnic boundaries. Consequently, even occasional instances of racism and interpersonal hostility may confirm the marginal status of minority users, for example, in the statement of an Asian carers support group, it reports that

> It is difficult to generalise as much of the care we have experienced has been really good, especially from the community nurses. However, it only takes a few bad experiences to confirm that Asians are not considered in the same way as others, this particularly relates to cultural awareness and sensitivity to our needs.

This is an important observation, for while anyone may have the regrettable experience of inadequate or inappropriate nursing or midwifery care, the reasons for this will not be the same for all. Underresourcing of a service or the random error of a tired professional may afflict any client, but racist exclusion or cultural marginalization are not likely to be the reason for service failure in relation to members of the majority population. Members of minority ethnic communities *do* have a legitimate sense of their unique relation to British society, which, among other things, arises from their cumulative experience of being members of cultural minorities in Britain. It is not reasonable, therefore, that the nursing professions should expect members of minority ethnic communities to suspend this sensibility solely in relation to their experience of health care. Nursing professions are not judged by the best practice of their most competent members, but rather by the routine performance of *all their* members. Thus, transcultural communicative competence must also include appropriate cultural knowledge and an empathetic attitude towards minority ethnic clients.

Examples of negative attitudes and hostility towards minority ethnic clients are regrettably not uncommon among the responses of the users.

- From a statement reporting the experience of Gujarati women: 'Many women reported very patronizing attitudes when they reached the hospital. Two women who spoke perfectly good English noticed that when their husbands, who were white, appeared their treatment changed; and he was spoken to.' (B.G.4)
- From the statement of an Asian carers group: 'It may not be the case that racism is actually present but if our everyday experience is that people see us as different then in a situation where we appear to be treated badly it is inevitable that this will act as further evidence of the fact that we are seen as different and somehow not quite as good. It is true that very few of our members report any instances of racism, at least they do not use the word, but they do talk about being upset at the attitudes they receive, ranging from the indifferent to the rude.' (A.C.S.2)

- From the report of a Chinese clients group: 'The client described her experiences of post-natal treatment, whereby she had requested a portable telephone three hours after giving birth to contact her husband. The nurse had told her that she had to get up and use the 'phone in the corridor. Again she made this request and again the 'phone was denied. Then another, "white", patient in the next bed made the same request, and the 'phone was given to her. The lady said that: "this was blatant prejudice and was completely unjustified".' (L.C.4)
- A comment from a Jewish mother who reported the response of the nursing staff when she wished for her baby boy to be circumcised: 'I was called barbaric and received other degrading comments from the nurses. I do accept that it is a barbaric operation for someone so small to undergo, but it is part of our religious needs.' (J.M.T.2)
- From an account by an Afro-Caribbean woman of the treatment of her husband while in hospital, which is a disturbing sequence of distressing incidents: 'In the first place he had no clothes on, everybody just going up and down just watching, looking at you. It was a disgrace, I used to feel embarrassed . . . Everybody in that ward had clothes on except him.' (A.C.I.3) Her account of his treatment ends with the statement, 'They couldn't give a damn about him; no respect.' (A.C.I.4)

Fortunately, these statements of hostility and negative attitudes are balanced by statements from all the minority ethnic communities interviewed, which report positive experiences of nursing and midwifery care in which the nursing staff were sensitive and caring. Some of these statements suggest that the nature of the context in which the interaction takes place may be important in facilitating such positive encounters. For example, an Asian carers group observed that:

> Many of our group get visits from community nurses and on the whole our experience here is very positive. When the nurses work with you on a one-to-one basis and are coming into your home, meeting your family, observing some of the customs and enjoying the food the whole interaction is different. Maybe because they have gained experience of the Asian community first hand they have more awareness of religion, food and our way of life. (A.C.S.4)

From an Afro-Caribbean carers group there is a complementary observation:

> On the other hand we should also mention that there have also been good experiences. The 'A' hospice and the 'B' hospital in 'Y' are smaller set-ups and very tranquil. You could not get better care than that we have witnessed there. Perhaps it has something to do with improved training. People's emotional needs and/or small institutions mean nurses are not so rushed and remain more constant. (A.C.C.4)

It is noticeable that both individual respondents and the statements of community groups contain references to the resource base of nursing care, and there is an awareness that not all instances of bad practice or lack of sensitive personal care stem from the individual prejudice or racism of practitioners. Overwork and stressed resources are acknowledged as significant determinants of the quality of nursing care. But equally those structural limitations within the health care service are not allowed to obscure the real hostility and lack of respect that minority ethnic clients may experience.

Recognizing and meeting cultural needs

For meeting the needs of minority ethnic clients, knowledge of their cultural beliefs and needs is an obvious element in the provision of nursing and midwifery care. While certain aspects of cultural beliefs and practices may be difficult to identify, and even more elusive to comprehend, from the outsider's perspective there are basic needs which are accessible and, while different in his or her particular case, part of a common experience of living. Food is one such need, which while a basic human need is the vehicle for a rich variety of ritual and meaning across the range of cultural mores (Douglas 1973; Harris 1977). Yet such a basic shared need is apparently one of the most frequent signs for ethnocentric thoughtlessness. Failure appropriately to meet the dietary expectation of minority ethnic clients ranges from a total non-recognition of their distinctive cultural expectations to a serious minded recognition of this as an issue in cross-cultural care, which is then confounded by a narrow stereotypical definition of 'what they eat'. Food recurs through the users' responses as a significant criterion in their evaluation of the quality of nursing and midwifery care. Here are ample examples of this concern.

- From the Afro-Caribbean community there is the observation that, 'Again there is an assumption that African-Caribbean people will eat English food, but the taste and ingredients of food are completely different. Whereas Asians in hospital will get Asian food provided, this is not the case for African Caribbean people.' (C.C.2)
- From the Asian community there is this summary of the significance of food: 'It is appreciated that both hospitals in X have made efforts to have some appropriate food in the form of the "ethnic menu". It has led to some difficulties. For example, because there is now this facility it is frowned on to bring our own food in; but often there are good reasons for our own dietary codes: say some things can be eaten only on special days; others are considered strength building. Also the hospital food does not offer much choice and if you don't happen to like the "ethnic menu" you may be stuck. There have also been examples of assuming that because someone looks Asian they will have the ethnic menu, but this is not always the first choice. We get the feeling that we ought to be grateful that this facility is there; and so we had better accept it good or bad!' (A.C.S.4)

- Food was also an issue among Jewish users, with the older generation particularly asserting its importance. One older user had had considerable experience of hospital treatment throughout England and had on all occasions either been asked or had asked for kosher food and received it. (J.N.H.5) Another reported that on being admitted to hospital she has been asked if she required kosher food but that 'in fact what I did eat was brought in by my relatives, then I could be sure of it.' (J.N.H.1)
- A Gujarati woman says of her father's experience: 'When my dad was in hospital, food was a problem and we had to take him food every day.' Another reports her experience of a midwifery ward thus: 'For Indian vegetarians they really need to look into it because although they have Indian food, it is inedible, I never had it while I was in hospital. I don't think they realize how much importance we put on food, and that it is not just about having nice food. It's also a question of the cultural beliefs that those things [particular foods] are strength giving and have other medical purposes.' (G.H.6)

Food, then, is but one of the more obvious concerns of minority ethnic communities as they expect their status as British citizens to be reflected in the quality of care they receive. Cultural expectations around notions of decency and privacy are recurrent in our users' data, and often reflect strong religious prescriptions and proscriptions around personal hygiene and body management. These norms vary widely across differing ethnic communities, but as fundamental aspects of a common human sense of one's own personhood are common to all societies. The data from interviews with minority ethnic users illustrate something of the range of concerns which the nursing professions must expect to address. For example:

- In Asian cultures, dignity, modesty and privacy, especially concerning the body, are absolutely essential, and this is particularly true of Asian women. However, we have no real hope of this improving as we are constantly being told that there is not enough space or staff to give us the privacy we so desperately want and need. Even when women have asked if they can see a woman doctor they have been told it depends on the availability. This can cause great anxiety and stress.' (A.C.S.2)
- This view was complemented by points made by a Gujarati women's group, who reported that 'Several women were upset by the number of internal examinations they had to have from different people, including male doctors. This was particularly upsetting; many women described this as being violated.' (B.G.4) 'Many women felt that there was insufficient privacy in getting changed or going for operations. One woman in hospital for suspected appendicitis had a finger thrust up her anus without explanation. She only found out later that this was a test for appendicitis. She was absolutely devastated, but the nurses just didn't seem to notice. When her husband came in later, she completely broke down.' (B.G.6)

- Among the Somali women interviewed there was a clear preference for female professionals to be their carers. Their experiences, however, varied. One woman reported that when stitches were put in following the delivery of her child, 'the doctor just came and did it ... They didn't ask her, so she didn't want to ask for herself.' (A.S.1) However, others were offered a choice, with one client saying that she was asked if she wanted a male or a female carer; and that, 'if there was a man, I would have objected.' (A.S.3)
- Even at very practical levels the exclusive majority infrastructure in an area may impinge upon providing appropriate care. 'It is commonly believed that deteriorating mental health is accompanied by deteriorating physical appearance and hygiene. Yet in the hospital where the project works there is no service for Black people to get skin and hair creams that they need. The hospital is in a white area where there are no Black shops. So unless a user has a family or friends who can do their shopping their appearance does deteriorate. Nurses should play a key role in encouraging people to improve and take pride in their appearance.' (A.C.M.H.3)

Concerns such as these expressed by minority ethnic users indicate how important appropriate cross-cultural knowledge is in enabling individual nursing professionals, *and* caring institutions, to anticipate the specific cultural needs and sensibilities of minority users. They confirm the evidence of prior studies, which have revealed the regrettable continuing failure of nursing and midwifery care to meet the cultural needs of minority ethnic users; yet they also reveal an existing process of change as specific institutions and particular individuals develop new competencies and sensibilities. While the user interviews contain instances of generic bad practice, and of racism and xenophobic intolerance, they also reveal a capacity within the nursing professions to accommodate to new demands and to provide care that is culturally sensitive and appropriate and that attracts very real user satisfaction.

The role of the minority ethnic professional

There is a theme that emerges within the users' data, which anticipates an issue that will be taken up again at a later point in this text. This concerns the role of minority ethnic nursing professionals in meeting the needs of their own minority ethnic communities. Clearly where user and carer share a common cultural background, even though there may be significant gender, caste, class and age differences, many of the difficulties of cross-cultural communication will be significantly minimized. Not surprisingly, therefore, this reality is echoed within the opinions of users who value the very real benefits that may follow from being cared for by a member of their own community. However, as we shall discuss below, there are dangers in allowing the ethnic matching of carer and user to be prescribed as the panacea to all the troubles facing the provision of nursing care in a multicultural society.

It should also be noted that the users' comments indicate sophisticated and concerned sensitivity regarding the role of the nursing professional in general. While individual members of the nursing professions may in some contexts be roundly condemned for their incompetence, ignorance or racism, this in no way can be interpreted as an expression of a commonly held view among members of the minority ethnic communities that the failings of the health care system are a simple consequence of the incompetence of individual professionals. There is ample indication of a willingness to temper criticism of practitioners, and indeed expectations made of them, by a critical consideration of the resource base within which they must work. At the level of individual interviewees this is shown in an appreciation of the stresses under which practitioners may be working. At the level of the considered view of minority ethnic community organizations, there may be a much more sophisticated analysis. For example:

> We end with a warning from Culled and Tyson that mirrors our own fears that despite some wonderful individuals and some excellent pockets of nursing care, the NHS is undergoing major reforms. While these reforms may prove an opportunity for delivering health care which is more appropriate and relevant to the needs of Britain's minority ethnic communities, there are also dangers that a more market orientated health care system may in fact reinforce and widen differentials. In examining the needs of Asian women and health it is insufficient to have funnel vision which looks from a power position in a wider society down the spout to the cultures for some answers. It is necessary to explore the political and social frameworks too of the health service to know where the real barriers are for nursing care to be more accessible, user friendly and free from discrimination. (B.G.8)

This perspective is one that may be fruitfully employed in any analysis of nursing and midwifery care in a multi-ethnic society; and it is in fact noticeably absent in some of the extant published research. For, while the nursing professions rightly require individual practitioners to take responsibility for the quality of their caring, it remains an inescapable truth that health care provision is highly responsive to government policy priorities and the allocation of scarce resources. We have seen in the literature the identification of 'blaming the victim' as a feature of some analysts' accounts of the health status of minority ethnic communities. Scapegoating health care professionals as the sole responsible cause of failures in health care delivery is equally inaccurate and unacceptable.

Conclusion

This chapter has established the necessity of locating contemporary health care needs and health care provision within a historical understanding of the development of contemporary multi-ethnic Britain. The ways in which central and local governments have sought to manage the challenges of ethnic diversity in post-war Britain constitute an essential element in shaping the repertoire of responses currently being employed in the management of ethnic diversity *per se*, and health care delivery specifically.

Ethnicity has been revealed to be a complex and changing phenomenon, which has important structural properties in addition to its more commonly understood significance for social identities. Through an examination of how cultural communicative competence may be conceptualized, something of the specific cultural knowledge required of nursing professionals has been revealed. And the complementary requirements of personal accommodation and flexibility that follow from anticipating the possibility of a generic intercultural communicative competence have been explored. The data from the interviews with minority ethnic users provide a concrete illustration of the importance of these necessary skills. Their absence not only causes personal offence and distress to minority clients, but may have serious consequences for diagnosis and treatment.

In moving on to examine the data generated by our research into how the professional education of nurses and midwives prepares them to be able to work with a multi-ethnic clientele, we invite the reader to bear in mind the issues raised in this chapter. There are powerful interpersonal dynamics, potentially loaded with a great deal of historical baggage, invoked in cross-cultural exchanges. The continuing marginalized position of many minority ethnic communities in Britain contributes not only to the determination of the health care needs of minority clients, but also to their perception of the quality of health care they receive. While individual professionals must accept their personal responsibility for equipping themselves to provide appropriate care to all clients, statutory and professional bodies must also be prepared to participate in the inherently political process of identifying health care needs and specifying those institutional conditions essential to enabling their members to fulfil their obligations to all their clients.

4

Preparing nursing professionals for multi-ethnic practice: a national overview

Introduction

The previous two chapters have served to highlight some of the complex demands that the nursing professions face in endeavouring to provide services which are responsive to the health care needs of a multi-ethnic society. Drawing upon the model of cultural and intercultural communicative competence proposed by Kim (1992), we have suggested a possible approach for moving towards appropriate care. However, considering Howell's (1982) framework for the development of competence, and the insights gleaned from minority ethnic users' experiences of nursing and midwifery care, it is legitimate to raise questions regarding the expertise and confidence of current practitioners in responding to the needs of minority ethnic clients. It is therefore timely to undertake a review of the current state of affairs by examining current pre-registration education.

As a research team we were challenged to seek to ascertain the extent to which pre-registration programmes of nursing and midwifery education equipped practitioners with the necessary competencies to meet the health care needs of minority ethnic communities. We began with a recognition that variations in ethnic demography would present different challenges to institutions in different parts of the country. We were therefore keen to gain a general overview of the full range of approaches taken in nursing and midwifery programmes; with this in mind we chose to undertake a survey by postal questionnaire of all institutions within England which offered the programmes with which we were particularly interested. However, we also recognized that a survey, although useful in presenting a national overview of the current situation, was likely to provide little in the way of an in-depth understanding of the issues which impact upon the preparation of nurses and midwives (see, for example, de Vaus (1985) for an examination of the survey method). In an attempt to overcome this deficit, we expanded upon the findings arising from the survey by undertaking an in-depth examination of three institutions in order to gain greater insight into the complexities of preparing practitioners to meet the needs of minority ethnic communities. In this chapter we present the national overview derived from the survey. We begin by providing a brief summary of the methods used in this stage of the research before moving on to consider the findings. In the following chapter we consider the three case study institutions in some detail.

Research methods

The national survey by postal questionnaire (Appendix 1) included all educational institutions which offered pre-registration diploma level programmes of adult and mental health nursing and midwifery and was designed to provide an overview of the extent to which practitioners are prepared to meet the health care needs of minority ethnic communities. Specifically, it examined the extent of the ethnic-related content of curricula, together with the methods and approaches used in teaching and learning, in both academic and practice settings. The questionnaire focused on five distinct areas which related to the overall aim of the project and explored a number of issues raised through our earlier review of the literature. These areas were:

- curriculum content and approaches;
- teaching and learning strategies;
- student learning opportunities;
- staff expertise in the areas of ethnicity and health;
- perceptions of the adequacy of classroom and practice experiences.

The questionnaire was designed to gather predominantly quantitative data, although there were a number of open questions whereby respondents could more freely express their opinions. Recognizing that the nursing programmes are divided into a common foundation programme and a subsequent branch programme, we chose to have separate questionnaires for each of these components, whereas for midwifery we had one questionnaire to cover the whole three-year programme. Thus we developed a total of four questionnaires, one for the common foundation programme, one for each of the two branch programmes in nursing and one for midwifery. The questionnaires were identical with the exception that each made explicit reference to the particular programme with which it was concerned.

The sample comprised 55 institutions offering pre-registration diploma level adult and mental health nursing programmes, 21 of which also offered pre-registration diploma level midwifery programmes. The cases to be surveyed constituted the education programmes within these institutions. Therefore institutions offering the nursing programmes received three questionnaires, while if, in addition, institutions offered a midwifery programme, they received a total of four questionnaires.

As the questionnaires were designed to seek detailed information on the curriculum, it was important to gather data from those individuals who were familiar with the particular programme and its delivery rather than more senior education managers, whose remit would be focused on organizational issues. Thus, although our formal approach to the institution was made to the principal (or equivalent), we requested that he or she forward the questionnaires to the most appropriate persons within the organization for completion. In view of this process, the characteristics of the respondents were largely unknown, other than by the professional speciality each individual represented.

The data arising from the questionnaires were subsequently coded using a framework developed by the researchers, with checks built in for assessing inter-rater reliability. Quantitative data were recorded on SPSS.Pc, and analysed using descriptive statistics. Qualitative data were counted for frequency and content analysed. Where qualitative data were quantified, these too were recorded on SPSS.Pc and in addition coded into categories to give a contextual understanding and clearer account of nursing and midwifery education in the field of minority ethnic issues.

Of the 55 institutions approached to participate in the survey, 91 per cent responded in whole or in part, i.e. they returned one or more questionnaires. The response rate for the common foundation programme was 73 per cent, whereas for the adult and mental health branch programmes responses were 64 and 67 per cent respectively. The response rate for the midwifery programme was 76 per cent. These response rates serve to provide an overall picture from which inferences can be drawn regarding the nature and extent of educational preparation for student nurses and midwives in order to equip them to work effectively in a multi-ethnic society.

The existing curriculum

One of the issues which may reasonably be addressed in an examination of the preparation of nurses and midwives to serve a multi-ethnic clientele is the question of identifying where within the taught curriculum the significance of ethnic diversity is addressed. This question has important implications, in that it may reveal that the issue is only addressed in isolated disciplinary areas, or it may be disproportionately perceived to be a subject incorporated within the social science input. Given the relative paucity of British literature on nursing and ethnicity, and the extensive visibility of ethnicity as a topic within the social sciences, this seemed a reasonable expectation. However, the data presented a more balanced and complex picture.

Respondents were asked to indicate the broad subject areas which they considered important in providing a knowledge base to prepare practitioners to meet the health care needs of minority ethnic communities (question 2). This question was open-ended, allowing respondents the opportunity to identify as many broad subject areas as they chose. In general, respondents

Table 4.1 The frequency with which broad subject headings were cited as being important in providing a knowledge base to prepare practitioners to meet the health care needs of minority ethnic communities (percentages)

	Common foundation programme n = 40	Adult branch programme n = 35	Mental health branch programme n = 37	Midwifery n = 17
Nursing/midwifery	93	89	78	100
Sociology	80	71	65	88
Social policy	33	26	16	25
Psychology	60	37	43	50
Other behavioural sciences	25	26	30	24
Biological sciences	38	29	5	38
Health studies	65	63	38	69
Community studies	18	11	14	19
Communication studies	43	34	30	13
Ethics, law and moral issues	30	43	27	25
Research	13	20	8	19

identified an average of four or five areas. However, the precise terminology used to describe particular subject areas was quite diverse, and it was necessary to group the specified subject areas into broader subject headings. In total, 11 broad subject headings were identified. Several of these could have been subsumed under the general heading 'behavioural sciences'. However, where a substantial number of respondents had specified a particular subject heading, a deliberate decision was taken to identify these individually; for example, psychology or sociology. Where a subject was mentioned less frequently it was subsumed under the heading 'other behavioural sciences'; examples of this included ethnicity and culture. The frequency with which respondents cited individual subject headings is shown in Table 4.1.

It should be noted that Table 4.1 only indicates the frequency with which a particular subject is mentioned, and does not give an indication of the perceived importance of the subject, or the extent to which it is included in the curriculum. Nevertheless, it is of note that for both the nursing and midwifery respondents, the professional subjects of nursing and midwifery, respectively, were most frequently cited. Subject areas within the broad behavioural sciences, including sociology, social policy and psychology, also featured prominently, as did the area of health studies. It is not appropriate to differentiate between the responses in the common foundation/branch programmes and in the midwifery programmes. The common foundation/branch programmes represent two separate parts of a total three-year nursing programme, whereas the midwifery programme is considered as a whole. Where it appears that certain subjects (for example, sociology or health studies) feature more frequently in midwifery programmes than they do in the common foundation or branch programmes, this may be because in respect of midwifery there is a summation between different components of the whole three-year programme. In other words, had the responses from the common foundation programmes and each of the two branch programmes been considered together, the picture for nursing programmes as a whole may have been more comparable with midwifery programmes.

Given some of the critical comments regarding the adequacy of the preparation of nurses for working with minority ethnic communities which arise shortly from the questionnaire survey, it is important to note here the positive significance of the findings in Table 4.1. A concern with the relevance of ethnic diversity has not been relegated to one particular subject area. While the data in Table 4.1 say nothing of the extent of coverage, or of the quality of the learning experience, they do indicate that all subject areas have a demonstrable capacity to introduce issues of ethnicity into their curricula. It is particularly significant that the core professional subject areas have been strongly identified as making a significant contribution. The behavioural sciences, with their long concern with the topic, are not surprisingly also significant contributors. Given its relevance to an understanding of health care delivery, it is perhaps regrettable that social policy has a relatively lower recorded contribution. And given the significance of community placements as a valuable source of acquiring the cross-cultural experience discussed elsewhere in the study, it is somewhat surprising that it should be seen as currently offering relatively little in the formal curriculum. In addition to identifying broad subject areas which respondents felt were important to enabling practitioners to meet the health care needs of minority ethnic groups, the data indicate that, in respect of nursing programmes, these subjects feature throughout the whole three-year programme rather than being specific to either the common foundation programme or one of the branch programmes. However, the majority of subject areas are cited slightly more frequently in the common foundation programme responses. This observation is not surprising, given the heavier weighting of theoretical studies to practical experience in the common foundation programmes compared to the branch programmes.

The following question (question 3) asked respondents to indicate, for each of the broad subject areas they had identified in the previous one (question 2), who was involved in teaching these components of the curriculum. For each subject area respondents could tick as many of the five categories as were appropriate. The categories identified were: nursing/midwifery lecturers from the approved institution; lecturers from other institutions; practitioners from health care settings; and members of minority ethnic groups drawn from the community. For example, in respect of nursing, they may indicate that both nursing lecturers and practitioners from health care settings were involved in teaching this subject area.

Table 4.2 Teaching responsibility for broad subject areas: common foundation programme (percentages)

	Nursing lecturers	Non-nursing lecturers	Lecturers from other institutions	Practitioners from health care settings	Members of minority ethnic groups in the community
Nursing n = 35	100	11.4	17.1	34.3	14.3
Sociology n = 31	94.5	35.5	35.5	9.7	6.5
Health studies n = 24	95.8	25.0	16.7	37.5	12.5
Psychology n = 23	95.7	34.8	13.0	13.0	0
Biological sciences n = 15	100	40.0	33.3	0	0

Table 4.3 Teaching responsibility for broad subject areas: adult branch programme (percentages)

	Nursing lecturers	Non-nursing lecturers	Lecturers from other institutions	Practitioners from health care settings	Members of minority ethnic groups in the community
Nursing n = 30	100	6.8	13.3	50.0	20.0
Sociology n = 24	95.8	25.0	29.2	33.3	16.7
Health studies n = 22	100	31.8	13.6	45.5	13.6
Psychology n = 12	91.7	16.7	25.0	33.3	8.3
Ethics, law and moral values n = 15	100	6.7	20.0	33.3	6.7

Tables 4.2 to 4.5 summarize the findings to this question. For each subject area the percentage of respondents who cited a particular category has been presented. Because respondents could identify more than one category for each subject area, the totals for each subject do not add up to 100 per cent. For example, in Table 4.2, all of the respondents (100 per cent) indicated that nursing lecturers were involved in teaching the nursing component

Table 4.4 Teaching responsibility for broad subject areas: mental health branch programme (percentages)

	Nursing lecturers	Non-nursing lecturers	Lecturers from other institutions	Practitioners from health care settings	Members of minority ethnic groups in the community
Nursing n = 29	100	17.2	13.8	51.7	10.3
Sociology n = 24	95.8	16.7	12.5	16.7	12.5
Health studies n = 15	93.3	53.3	20.0	40.0	13.3
Psychology n = 16	87.5	25.0	31.3	6.3	12.6
Ethics, law and moral values n = 10	100	30.0	40.0	40.0	10.0

Table 4.5 Teaching responsibility for broad subject areas: midwifery programme (percentages)

	Midwifery lecturers	Non-midwifery lecturers	Lecturers from other institutions	Practitioners from health care settings	Members of minority ethnic groups in the community
Nursing n = 16	100	25.0	25.0	50.0	31.3
Sociology n = 14	78.6	71.4	42.9	21.4	14.3
Health studies n = 11	90.9	54.6	36.4	36.4	36.4
Psychology n = 8	100	75.0	50.0	62.5	25.0
Biological sciences n = 6	100	75.0	50.0	33.3	33.3

and 34 per cent of them indicated that practitioners from health care settings were also involved. Because of the relatively small number of responses for each subject area, only the five most frequently cited subjects for each programme have been presented.

Although the data identify the broad range of people who are involved in teaching the ethnic-related component of the curriculum, responses do not indicate what proportion of the teaching is undertaken by a particular category of teacher. However, responses confirm that nursing and midwifery lecturers feature prominently, taking on a somewhat generalist teaching role. This finding is open to contradictory interpretations. At one level, it is desirable and admirable that in any formal teaching in a professional context those teaching the material have experience of putting it into practice and making it relevant to practice. At another level, it may be a source of anxiety that nursing and midwifery lecturers feel competent to teach over such a wide range of subjects. Anecdotal evidence suggests that some of this apparent competence may in some instances be engendered more by the resourcing pressures in education institutions than by the wide-ranging competencies of specific staff. Indeed, given the data to be discussed below regarding the limited extent to which staff have been facilitated in acquiring competence to teach the ethnic-related parts of the curriculum, we may reasonably declare a general anxiety in respect of this element of teaching.

Tables 4.2 to 4.5 also reveal interesting findings relating to the role of lecturers from other institutions. While there is no overall consistency in their contribution to particular subjects across the four tables, they clearly can play a very significant role in servicing particular subjects in particular institutions. While this arrangement may enable students to be taught by staff with real expertise in the subject, it raises questions regarding the construction of a coherent curriculum. Externally employed staff often have their priorities defined for them by their principal employer. They may not be available for staff meetings in the education institution, and may have difficulty in meaningfully identifying with the professional ethos of the programme.

When, however, a programme is seeking to develop a coherent response to a new professional challenge, such as the present challenge of addressing the needs of a multi-ethnic clientele, these tensions may prove major obstacles to achieving such coherence in approach and content. Additionally, given the concern expressed later regarding the apparently minimalist contact between education and practice settings, staff from other institutions may be even more easily isolated from contact with practice settings.

Tables 4.2 to 4.5 also suggest that individuals from minority ethnic communities are not routinely seen as a source of expertise which may be appropriately drawn upon in developing a curriculum that is appropriate to a multi-ethnic society. Clearly, a tokenistic practice of bringing professionals or users from minority ethnic communities into programmes where their community's existence is routinely absent from the core curriculum is hardly justifiable. Nor is it appropriate to use such expertise as a means of absolving the subject specialist from any responsibility to develop his or her own expertise. But as the minority ethnic community voluntary and independent sector becomes an increasingly important element in the system of health and social care provision in Britain, nursing professionals need to be familiar with the range of services they offer, and the repository of expertise they collectively constitute. And, as has been argued in Chapter 3, the voice of the user is an essential source of feedback and insight for all practitioners.

In order to focus on specific content relating to the health care needs of minority ethnic communities, respondents were required to complete a menu question (question 5). This question comprised 12 topics identified from a review of health and nursing literature. Respondents were asked to tick whether these topics were 'not included', 'briefly mentioned', 'introduced and given some attention' or 'given extensive coverage'. In addition, space was included to enable respondents to add further topics they felt had not been included in the menu. Few respondents made suggestions; however, of those who did, their additional topics bore such close resemblance to those identified on the menu of 12, that these additional topics were coded into the main menu and interpreted as one question (Figures 4.1 to 4.4).

The responses summarized in Figures 4.1 to 4.4 tended to indicate that extensive coverage of any of the topics relating to the health care needs of minority ethnic communities was unlikely. If readers examine the relative degree of attention given to each topic they may feel that one disturbing aspect of the data is the extent to which some topics are 'not included' or 'only briefly mentioned'. If these two categories are summated it is reassuring to see that concepts of 'ethnicity, culture and race' are usually not neglected, whereas the health-related topics of 'health beliefs', 'ethnic minorities' health needs' and 'ethnic minorities' access to health services' seem more likely to receive scant attention in a significant number of programmes. This situation would also seem to be even more evident in relation to discussion of the social and political contexts of ethnic minorities' health and health care provision. Given the fundamental relevance of an understanding of minority ethnic communities' health beliefs to the provision of appropriate care this is not a comforting observation. Equally, we have argued that health care needs and provision must be understood within a broader social and political framework. Particularly since the response category 'introduced and given some attention' allows for respondents to be economical with the truth in determining for themselves what constitutes 'some attention', the use of the category may be somewhat inflated by the 'social desirability effect' as respondents seek to present their activities in the best possible light. Consequently, a more demanding examination of the data may result from focusing upon the response category 'given substantial attention'.

Only a minority of respondents are able to indicate that these topics are dealt with in depth; and in many instances only one-fifth or fewer of the respondents are able to respond in this way. Even a conservative interpretation of these data must lead to anxiety regarding the adequacy of education programmes in these fundamental building blocks of professional competence to address practice in a society characterized by ethnic diversity.

Figure 4.1 The extent to which selected topics featured within the common foundation programme curriculum

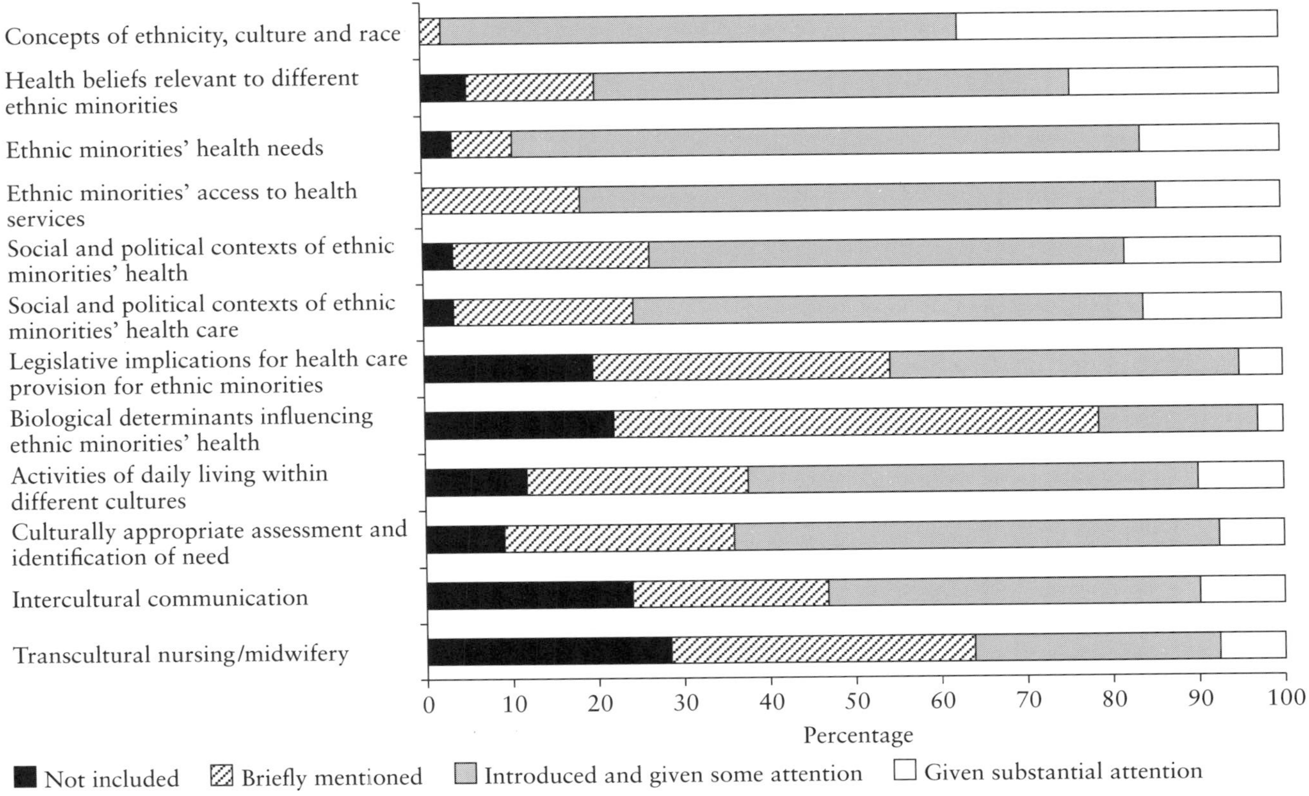

Concepts of ethnicity, culture and race
Health beliefs relevant to different ethnic minorities
Ethnic minorities' health needs
Ethnic minorities' access to health services
Social and political contexts of ethnic minorities' health
Social and political contexts of ethnic minorities' health care
Legislative implications for health care provision for ethnic minorities
Biological determinants influencing ethnic minorities' health
Activities of daily living within different cultures
Culturally appropriate assessment and identification of need
Intercultural communication
Transcultural nursing/midwifery
0
10
20
30
40
50
60
70
80
90
100
Percentage
Not included
Briefly mentioned
Introduced and given some attention
Given substantial attention

Figure 4.2 The extent to which selected topics featured within the adult branch programme curriculum

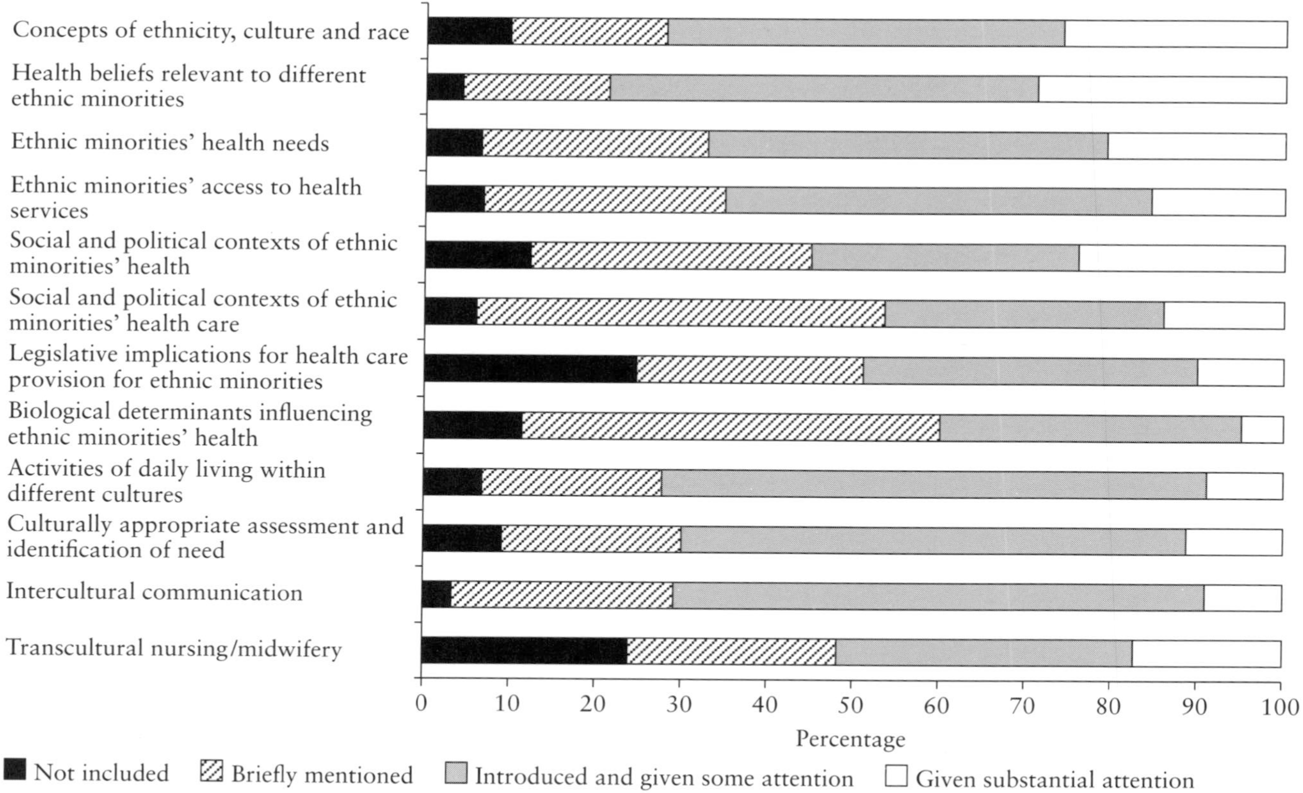

Concepts of ethnicity, culture and race
Health beliefs relevant to different ethnic minorities
Ethnic minorities' health needs
Ethnic minorities' access to health services
Social and political contexts of ethnic minorities' health
Social and political contexts of ethnic minorities' health care
Legislative implications for health care provision for ethnic minorities
Biological determinants influencing ethnic minorities' health
Activities of daily living within different cultures
Culturally appropriate assessment and identification of need
Intercultural communication
Transcultural nursing/midwifery
0
10
20
30
40
50
60
70
80
90
100
Percentage
Not included
Briefly mentioned
Introduced and given some attention
Given substantial attention

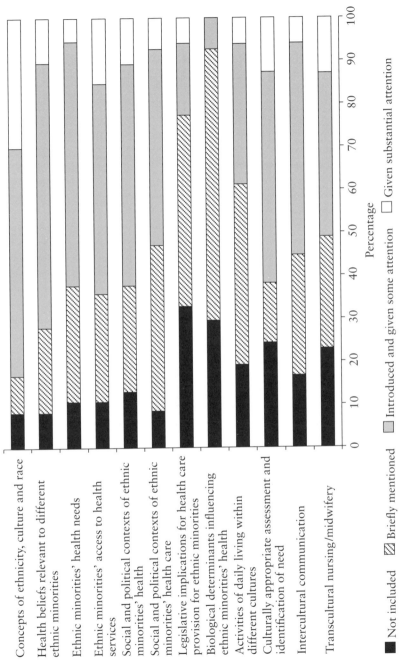

Figure 4.3 The extent to which selected topics featured within the mental health branch programme curriculum

Figure 4.4   The extent to which selected topics featured within the midwifery curriculum

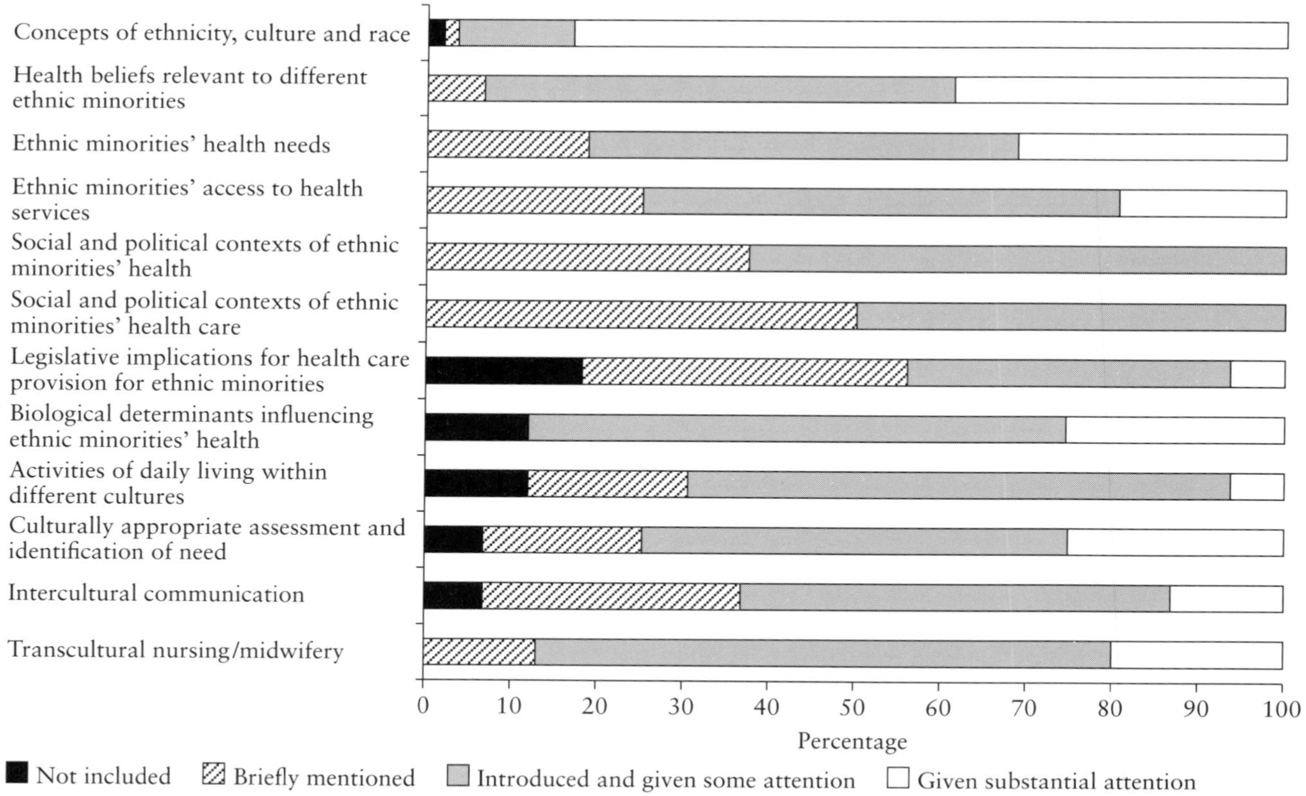

Concepts of ethnicity, culture and race

Health beliefs relevant to different ethnic minorities

Ethnic minorities' health needs

Ethnic minorities' access to health services

Social and political contexts of ethnic minorities' health

Social and political contexts of ethnic minorities' health care

Legislative implications for health care provision for ethnic minorities

Biological determinants influencing ethnic minorities' health

Activities of daily living within different cultures

Culturally appropriate assessment and identification of need

Intercultural communication

Transcultural nursing/midwifery

Percentage

■ Not included   ▨ Briefly mentioned   ▨ Introduced and given some attention   □ Given substantial attention

Of course, one legitimate response to these data might be to ask the question: 'what would constitute adequate coverage of these topics?' Anticipating some of our findings from the case studies, we are aware of the fact that teaching staff already experience the curriculum as overcrowded and heavily pressurised. This allows for an apparently reasonable resistance to demands that additional material should be incorporated into this already unrealistically packed curriculum. We would suggest that a very obvious way of countering this resistance lies in Table 4.1 and our discussion of it: namely, the extent to which across the whole curriculum different subject areas have already been identified by staff as appropriate vehicles for introducing students to issues of ethnicity and health care delivery in a multi-ethnic context. Thus the solution lies in developing students' understanding of existing concepts and issues within the curriculum by introducing ethnicity as a comparative variable. By permeating the curriculum with a conscious awareness of ethnicity and 'race' as relevant variables in relation to a wide range of concepts and topics it is possible to do more than 'briefly mention' or just 'give some attention' to very significant topics relevant to competence in practising in a multi-ethnic society. This is an issue of curriculum planning, resource availability and management, and the political will to address this challenge meaningfully. Clearly, it is not a simple matter, but nor is it an irresolvable task. However, in the absence of a willingness to address this challenge, failure is inevitable; and we must record that some of the returned questionnaires were unambiguous in their willingness to declare ethnicity as an irrelevance to them, or, expressed more bluntly, a blatant hostility to being expected to address the issue.

The data in Figures 4.1 to 4.4 indicate a degree of variation between the responses of different programmes. While we would be reticent to read too much into these variations, it is worthwhile encouraging readers to develop their own hypotheses. For example, it is noticeable over the range of topics covered in these figures that midwifery appears to give more detailed coverage of the topics than the adult or the mental health branch programmes. However, as noted above, these two branch programmes need to be seen in relation to the input of the common foundation programme. Consequently, it may be that the appropriate interpretation of the data is that within the adult and mental health branch programmes there may be a tendency for the coverage of topics related to the health of minority ethnic communities to diminish in the transition from the common foundation to the branch programme.

It is interesting to observe that 'intercultural communication' appears to be more widely represented within the curriculum than 'transcultural nursing/midwifery'. This is an interesting observation, for it suggests a number of possibilities. One is that the expertise in 'intercultural communication' is more available across the range of teaching staff, including the behavioural science specialists, whereas transcultural nursing is a more arcane specialism of nursing lecturers. Another possibility has more to do with the teaching staffs' perceptions of the connotations of particular labels; and it is possible that 'transcultural nursing/midwifery' may be perceived as being more closely associated with a more narrowly defined North American phenomenon, associated with the work of Leininger (1978, 1990), rather than the broader perspective which is beginning to feature in the British literature (McGee 1994; Papadopoulos *et al.* 1994a). In either case, the distinct visibility of transcultural midwifery in the midwifery response remains to be accounted for.

Figures 4.3 and 4.4, in their representation of the visibility of 'biological determinants influencing ethnic minorities' health', throw up a further interesting observation in relation to the relative significance of this topic in midwifery and its particular invisibility in the mental health branch curriculum. Among other possibilities, this implies that historical controversies surrounding the connection between biologically determined mental illness and 'race' (Ineichen 1989) may not be being considered. Furthermore, the data in Figures 4.1 to 4.3 may suggest that the current contentious debate around consanguinity (Ahmad 1996) as an explanatory variable may not be being addressed, and that the linkages of ethnic category and haemoglobinopathies (Anionwu 1993) may not be fully examined.

While aspects of curriculum content were revealed in Figures 4.1 to 4.4, it was important to examine a more general issue relating to the incorporation of ethnicity into the curriculum. Information regarding the different approaches taken to integrating issues relating to the health care needs of minority ethnic communities into curricula was collected using an open-ended question (question 4) in which two distinct options of permeation or specific units were suggested (McGee 1992).

Responses were initially content analysed, coded into five groups, and a frequency count undertaken (Figure 4.5), showing 'permeation' to be the

Figure 4.5 Curriculum strategies employed

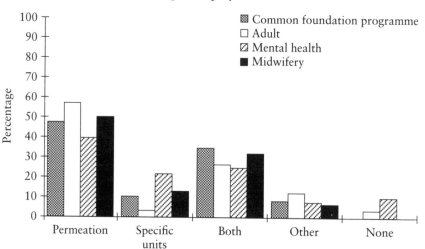

most popular approach. However, the descriptions of permeation and specific units cited by McGee (1992) proved difficult to employ as a framework. It became clear from analysis of the nature of responses that some discrepancies existed between the meanings attributed by the respondents to the different approaches.

Where specific input was described, there were variations in how this was delivered, and for how long. Specific sessions were usually said to be offered in the sociology theme. In some instances this constituted one or two sessions occurring at a predetermined point in the common foundation, branch or midwifery programmes, or a number of sessions delivered intermittently throughout the three-year nursing and midwifery programmes. The latter were considered by other respondents as evidence of permeation. Some respondents described a combination of the two approaches, which next to permeation was the second most popular response. The responses classed as 'other' tended to refer to confusion between curriculum approaches and teaching strategies, leading respondents to describe teaching sessions. Clearly, the varied interpretations of this qualitative question undermine the ability to draw responsible conclusions from the data, other than a general suggestion that input is likely to be integrated within programme content, rather than taught as a discreet module. However, the data support the position currently advocated by the small body of literature concerning the incorporation of ethnic-related content within nursing curricula (Byerly 1977; McGee 1992; Papadopoulos *et al.* 1994b).

Overall, the questionnaire survey of curricula content has generated a sense that many programmes have begun to address the issue of how to prepare members of the nursing professions to work in a multi-ethnic society. However, the data leave no room for complacency. A number of institutions felt able to declare that there are no minority ethnic communities in their locality; hence it was not an issue for them. Other responses very strongly suggested that a barely tokenistic acknowledgement of the challenge of ethnic diversity had been put in place. On the other hand, a few institutions were quite clearly committed to attempting to ensure that their curriculum is appropriate to preparing nurses and midwives for cross-cultural practice. The range of institutional response is wide, yet the model position is not one with which the nursing professions could be content to defend as an adequate professional preparation for practice.

Teaching and learning strategies

In addition to examining curricula content, the survey sought to reveal what teaching and learning strategies were being employed in order to introduce students to the issue of ethnic diversity and the development of competencies that would fit them to work with a multi-ethnic clientele. Consequently, a question was introduced to elicit information about innovative teaching and learning strategies that were used in developing components of the curriculum which prepared students to meet the health care needs of minority ethnic communities (question 8). The response to this question indicated that there was a balance between taught components, practice-based initiatives and a combination of the two. In the common foundation programme, innovative strategies were more likely to be part of a taught component, reflecting the emphasis on classroom teaching in the early part of the overall nursing programme. In midwifery responses, combined practice-based and classroom initiatives were more widely cited.

Approximately half of the respondents completed this item. Where topics and teaching strategies were suggested, these were coded into the following categories: interpersonal/communication skills, spiritual/religious needs, cultural understanding and health promotion. Of these, the category communication/interpersonal skills was by far the largest, followed by spiritual/religious needs. Teaching strategies employed varied across each of the above categories. These are summarized as follows:

Case studies	care study, case histories
Discussion	discussion groups, student presentations, question and answer sessions, seminars, small group discussions
Experiential learning	cooking, demonstrations, developing and using a teaching package, experiential exercises, interactive video, role play
Group work	group work, group presentations, workshops
Lecture	lectures, visiting speakers
Reflective learning	critical incident technique, learning diaries
Student directed learning	project work, self-directed learning, study guides, work sheets
Other	conferences, poster presentations.

Although these methods were used in each of the above subject categories, patterns emerged whereby experiential methods were used more widely to teach communication skills. The development and use of teaching packs were favoured in health promotion modules, while the category 'other' encompassed approaches to establishing an understanding of the full spectrum of the lifestyle and health needs of minority ethnic communities.

In determining who held the responsibility for overseeing the preparation of students in areas of ethnicity, respondents were required first of all to indicate whether such a named person existed in their institution by means of a 'yes' or 'no' response. Where respondents answered 'yes' they were requested to describe the persons' role(s), and give their job title(s) (question 10). Percentages of 'yes' responses were low (Figure 4.6).

It was clear from the descriptive responses that responsibility generally rests with nursing/midwifery teachers having a personal interest and commitment to the subject. Therefore, where named individuals were cited, this was usually because those persons had acquired the reputation for

Figure 4.6 Percentage of institutions identifying a named teacher with responsibility for overseeing the preparation of practitioners to meet the health care needs of minority ethnic communities

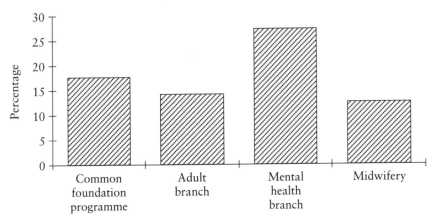

specializing in the area through informal networks. More senior teachers were likewise cited as taking on the responsibility for this aspect of the curriculum, either through their role in managing the delivery of curriculum content or through personal interest. None of the suggested individuals based within an institution held a role title which identified them as specialists in the health needs of minority ethnic communities. However, two respondents referred to individuals employed by their local trusts; one a 'cultural advisor', the other a 'clinical nurse specialist: ethnic minorities' issues'. In both instances the specialists were called upon to teach and advise on programmes. However, the overall conclusion is that institutions have predominantly failed to indicate a managerial responsibility for promoting the multi-ethnic relevance of nursing or midwifery education by identifying a member of staff to take the lead through providing a coordinating function across the curriculum. This managerial inertia is compounded by the dearth of evidence of institutions providing or supporting staff development in this area (Figure 4.10).

Anticipating somewhat the discussion of staff expertise which follows below, it should be noted that when respondents were asked whether any individual members of the teaching staff had undergone specific staff development to prepare them to deliver the ethnicity related aspects of the curriculum (question 11), the responses reflected in Figure 4.10 are far from reassuring. They suggest a managerial perception that this is not a priority issue, or at least that it is a recently identified issue. Linked with the discussion of Figure 4.6, it lends credence to one of the findings from the case study analysis: namely, that the possession and acquisition of teaching competence in this area is currently predominantly regarded as an individual choice/commitment, rather than as a necessary part of managerial resource planning.

Figure 4.7 Percentage of programmes providing the opportunity for students to undertake a detailed study of a client group from a different culture to their own

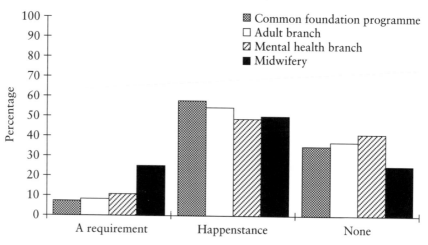

Students' learning opportunities

As an indicator of opportunities available for students to develop their knowledge of the health care needs of minority ethnic communities, respondents were asked a two-staged question (question 7) about whether students undertook a detailed study of a client or client group from a different culture to their own as part of their programme which might provide them with valuable insights in relating the taught components of the curriculum to client care (Lynam 1992; DeSantis 1994). Following the aforementioned format regarding teaching strategies, a 'yes/no' answer provided the filter for a further open-ended question enabling respondents to elaborate on the affirmative (Figure 4.7). It became evident when we were coding this question that respondents who indicated that there was the opportunity for students to undertake such a detailed study differentiated between this being a requirement for all students, or the students' own choice. The responses were subsequently coded into three categories: a requirement, happenstance or none.

Many respondents identified this question as referring to a written piece of assessed work. The most common opportunity for students to undertake a detailed study of a client or client group occurred through a neighbourhood study or client care study. The students, without exception, could choose the client or group, and therefore, although it was described as common for students to be attracted towards the study of minority ethnic communities, this tended to be by happenstance.

Exceptions to this constituted studies specifically designed to enable students to understand the needs of minority ethnic communities; for example,

Figure 4.8 Percentage of programmes in which the learning outcomes for practice placements make explicit reference to meeting the needs of clients from minority ethnic communities

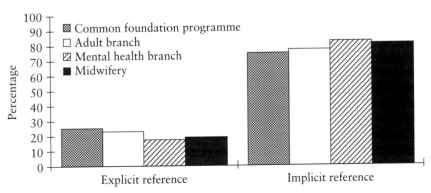

a 'cultural perspectives project' in which students could study the history, lifestyle, education, religious practices, health care needs and activities of daily living of people from one minority ethnic community of their choice. An alternative took a comparative approach, whereby students compared the lives of people in different local areas, encompassing a study of class and culture. Other opportunities involved non-assessed practice initiatives with community health professionals, where students met specialists providing health care for minority ethnic and traveller populations.

Although, as is clear in Figure 4.7, students generally are unlikely to be required to conduct such a specialized study, in a quarter of midwifery programmes such projects are compulsory, suggesting a higher profile for minority ethnic issues among student midwives than among student nurses. This is consistent with our interpretation of the distinctive profile of midwifery in Figures 4.1 to 4.4. However, when compared to results from a closed question (question 12) investigating whether ethnic minorities' issues were implicit or explicit in respect of the learning outcomes for practice placements (Figure 4.8), slightly fewer midwifery programmes were using such explicit learning outcomes. This may suggest that in depth studies are not necessarily practice-based.

On the whole, the approach taken in the common foundation programme regarding learning outcomes for practice placements does not significantly differ from that taken in the branch programmes. In each of the programmes, learning outcomes relating to the care of minority ethnic clients tend to be implicit, despite the educational emphasis on achieving specific objectives in the early part of the nursing programmes. However, the results are in keeping with those relating to curriculum strategies, in which 'permeation' was shown to be a favoured strategy for including the needs of minority ethnic communities in nursing and midwifery education.

To some extent, this pattern is reflected in the small number of practice

Figure 4.9 Percentage of programmes providing practice placements specifically intended to develop culturally sensitive care

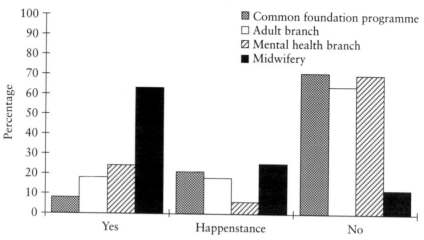

placements for students which are designated as offering a specific opportunity to develop care sensitive to the needs of minority ethnic communities (question 13, Figure 4.9).

Where specific placements were identified, they were predominantly maternity care placements. Throughout the four programmes, designated placements tended to be located in the community rather than hospital settings; for example, placements with community psychiatric nursing teams or with midwives operating in geographical areas with a high minority ethnic population, and placements at day centres catering for minority ethnic clients, including a community initiative to support Afro-Caribbean users. The limited number of hospital-based placements tended to be confined to haemoglobinopathy clinics and haematology units.

In general, respondents located in areas with large minority ethnic communities commented on how frequently students came into contact with minority ethnic clients, in both hospital and community placements. Those replying from areas where the minority ethnic population is not as visible stated that this low visibility, together with the lack of specialist placements, made it difficult for them to enable the students to link the theoretical studies of minority ethnic health issues to practice. One respondent commented on how the team in her institution would need to consider looking for placements outside of the immediate locality, in order to provide students with the experience of caring for minority ethnic clients.

Students' learning opportunities are consequently constrained by practice placement resources, although, additionally, guidance towards pursuing knowledge from a theoretical perspective appears to be haphazard. It is largely the case that students negotiate their own opportunities based upon broad criteria for course work, or by meeting patients from minority

Figure 4.10 Percentage of programmes where members of teaching staff have undertaken specific staff development

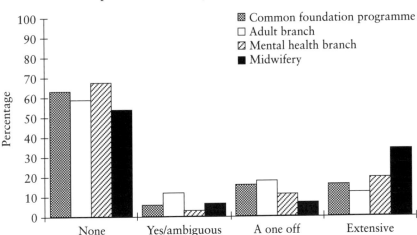

ethnic communities in their clinical work, adding to the haphazard nature in which formal education in the area was seen to be delivered. However, where the study of an alternative culture is required, these projects take an imaginative approach and, for example, strive to link bio-psycho-social concepts of ethnicity and health care needs to professional practice.

Staff expertise in the areas of ethnicity and health

As noted above, the amount and range of teaching relating to the health care needs of minority ethnic communities cannot reasonably be considered without placing this in the context of staff expertise in the area. Respondents were asked to give details of specific staff development based upon a 'yes/no' response, followed by a detailed description (question 11). Affirmative and negative responses were counted. However, in some instances respondents had replied in the affirmative, but not provided a description of what form their staff development had taken. These replies were classed as 'yes, ambiguous' answers. Remaining descriptions were coded into 'one off' experiences, i.e. the equivalent of attending a three-day workshop, or 'extensive', i.e. the equivalent of attending a full module in a course of higher education or through research (Figure 4.10).

Respondents referred to members of staff who had pursued modules relating to ethnicity, culture or 'race' while studying for a degree, at both bachelors and masters levels. There was also an indication that where personal interests have been pursued in higher education, those staff continue to raise the awareness of colleagues by offering study days or reviewing literature for circulation. Of these respondents, midwifery teachers were more

likely to have undergone extensive staff development. Alternative opportunities for staff to become prepared to teach the ethnic-related aspects
of the curriculum involved study days, both internal to the institution and
by linking with outside agencies. Many respondents referred to these days
as covering topics such as equal opportunities (which tended to be compulsory) and 'race' awareness.

The data also suggest a tendency for teachers from minority ethnic communities to be considered to be expert in this field by virtue of their ethnic
identity. Furthermore, their expertise is considered to encompass in-depth
knowledge and understanding of all minority ethnic communities. This is
a phenomenon which is echoed in the data from the case studies; and it
is something which we will discuss more extensively below. In summariz-
ing the implications of Figure 4.10, it would be reasonable to assert that
there appear to be pockets of interest rather than a national drive towards
achieving culturally sensitive understanding among teachers. The responses
to this question indicate a degree of voluntarism in the pursuit of professional development in this area and suggests a considerable need for
educational management to take a more proactive role in promoting staff
development.

Respondents' opinions of the adequacy of classroom and clinical experiences

Two open-ended elements of the questionnaire (question 14) examined the
extent to which respondents thought that students were sufficiently prepared through their course work and practice placements to meet successfully the health care needs of minority ethnic communities. The responses
categorized as 'yes' or 'no' were unqualified assertions that course work, or
practice placements, did or did not prepare students adequately. A 'qualified yes' constituted responses which were positive about some elements of
the course, but highlighted parts which were inadequate.

Figure 4.11 depicts the quantitative data regarding course work. Of the
positive responses, midwife teachers were most satisfied with the outcome
of the course work component of the curriculum, with the highest level of
agreement among all respondents centred on a 'qualified yes'. Respondents
expressed less certainty about practice placements.

These responses suggest an awareness that at present professional training for nursing and midwifery is not able to assure potential employers
that they are producing staff who are fit for purpose in a multi-ethnic
society. This perceived state of play in relation to the taught element of the
programmes of professional training is entirely consistent with the findings
from the survey reviewed over the past few pages. While some institutions
have made concerted efforts to develop appropriate curricula, many more
have begun to address the issue in an uncoordinated piecemeal manner,

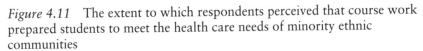

Figure 4.11 The extent to which respondents perceived that course work prepared students to meet the health care needs of minority ethnic communities

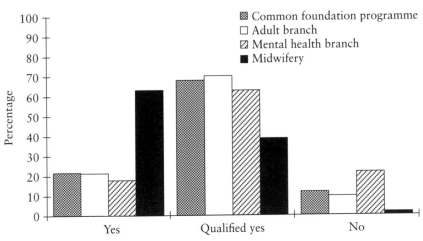

and too many may not yet have accepted that this is an area of competence which they must address. This raises important and unavoidable questions about the role of professional bodies in validating programmes, and of commissioning consortia in exercising their power in funding training.

From the earlier consideration of the limited availability of practice placements it is hardly surprising that a significant proportion of respondents voiced some reservations as to the extent to which students were sufficiently prepared through their practice placements to meet the health care needs of minority ethnic communities (Figure 4.12).

A major point reiterated in the qualitative analysis of this question was the variability of practice learning opportunities. Respondents indicated that some students might have more opportunity to develop proficiency in this area than others dependent upon the availability of suitable placements. Furthermore, the quality of the placements was seen to depend upon the quality of supervision students received, which some teachers found difficult to monitor. Those respondents who considered that practice placements did not prepare students adequately identified two main reasons. First, their local area was not known to be highly populated by minority ethnic communities, and therefore specialist placements were not available and students were not likely to encounter minority ethnic clients in their day-to-day practice in more general placements. Second, although the students might come across people with different ethnic identities, the extent to which they were able to link theory with practice was dependent upon the students' own personal interests or the possibility of colleagues drawing their attention to different values and beliefs, rather than through any planned systematic learning process.

Figure 4.12 The extent to which respondents perceived that practice placements prepared students to meet the health care needs of minority ethnic communities

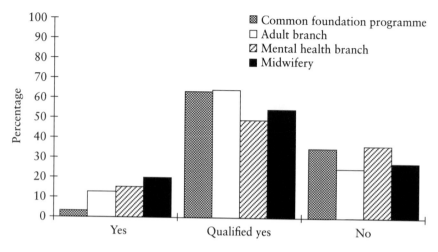

Conclusion

The findings from the national survey of the curricula of pre-registration nursing and midwifery programmes have served to provide an overview of the extent to which the programmes prepare practitioners to meet the health care needs of minority ethnic communities. We will return to a number of the issues raised from this stage of the study in Chapter 7 when we consider the findings of the survey alongside those of the case studies. However, for the present, and by way of summary, it would appear that although it is apparent that many programmes have begun to address the issue of how to prepare practitioners to work in a multi-ethnic society, there is no place for complacency. On the one hand a few institutions are quite clearly committed to attempting to ensure that their curriculum is appropriate and effective in equipping practitioners with the necessary competencies. However, other responses were less encouraging. A number of institutions appeared to suggest a minimal and tokenistic response to the challenge of ethnic diversity. Yet others apparently abdicated responsibility for addressing these issues on account of the fact that they considered that there were no minority ethnic communities in their locality and therefore had little cause to include it within their curricula.

The findings have also served to highlight the somewhat happenstance nature of learning about the needs of minority ethnic communities. There appears to be no guarantee, even in institutions which indicate a strong commitment to addressing these issues, that all students will have the opportunity to examine the needs of minority ethnic communities in sufficient depth during the course of their programmes. One of the reasons for this is clearly linked to resources and in particular to the limited availability of suitable practice placements. However, it would also appear that guidance towards pursuing knowledge from a theoretical perspective is also haphazard. Few programmes make it a requirement for all students to address these issues through formal course work. Rather, it is left largely to the individual students to negotiate their own opportunities based upon broad criteria for course work and their personal interests. While this amount of flexibility is commendable in allowing students a degree of autonomy in the learning process, it does provide the opportunity for some students, if they so wish to choose not to address the issue at all. Such an approach seriously brings into question whether at present pre-registration programmes of nursing and midwifery education provide an adequate preparation for working in a multi-ethnic society.

5

Institutions, pedagogy and practice: the case studies

Introduction

The findings from the survey outlined in Chapter 4 have served to provide an account of current pre-registration nursing and midwifery education and give an indication of the extent to which programmes equip practitioners with the competencies to work in a multi-ethnic context. However, while the findings provide a broad overview, they say little about the actual experiences of those involved directly in the design and delivery of education programmes, either as students or those who support the students' learning. In order to gain a fuller understanding of the complexities of preparing nurses and midwives to provide care in a multi-ethnic society, we sought to undertake a detailed examination of three institutions which provided the programmes with which we were interested. These comprehensive case studies provide a much richer account than the survey data were able to impart and help to furnish an understanding of the complex and sometimes competing factors which influence the design, delivery and outcomes of pre-registration nursing and midwifery education. In this chapter we present our analysis of the data arising from the case studies and in doing so illustrate some of the strategies being employed to enable students and practitioners to work effectively within a multi-ethnic society. Through placing our examination of nursing and midwifery curricula within the wider organizational context, we are able to gain helpful insights into the impact that a particular organization's ethos exerts on educational delivery. However, while the particularities of each case study are in their own way unique, we also identify a number of common practices and concerns shared across the three institutions. We begin with a brief account of the research methods employed before presenting the findings.

Research methods

Yin (1993, 1994) highlights the benefits of using a case study approach to investigate a phenomenon within its real-life context and considers it a particularly useful strategy when the boundaries between the phenomenon and context are not clearly evident. As we identified in Chapter 1, the phenomena we were examining (programmes of nursing and midwifery education) were intricately bound up with the broader health and education context; and it was thought that by using a case study approach we would be able to examine the complex relationship of nursing and midwifery education to this broader arena.

The aim of the case studies was therefore to gain more insight into the curriculum as it was designed, as it was delivered and as it was experienced by the main parties involved. To this end we were particularly interested in teasing out what were perceived to be the strengths and limitations of the particular programmes we were examining and what factors influenced their design and delivery. Acknowledging that students learn in both the academic and practice settings, it was necessary to extend the case studies beyond the particular education institution to include local NHS trusts in which students gained their practice experiences.

In order to gain insight into the perceptions and experiences of those involved in the programmes, we used qualitative methods of data collection. Focus group interviews were undertaken with separate groups of students, teachers, newly qualified practitioners and experienced qualified nurses and midwives, who acted as mentors/assessors to students for each of the three programmes we were examining. The same agenda was used for each of the focus groups and provided the opportunity to explore in some degree of detail the participants' perceptions of the strengths and limitations of the curriculum in terms of equipping practitioners to meet the needs of minority ethnic communities (see Appendix 2). We refer the reader to Morgan (1993) and Krueger (1994) for a detailed account of the focus group method.

In order to supplement the data arising from the focus group discussions, individual semi-structured interviews were undertaken with senior education managers and service managers involved with the programmes in each of the case study locations. The interviews followed very closely the agenda used for the focus groups, with the exception that we took the opportunity to seek some contextual information relating to the institutions themselves and to explore issues relating to the recruitment of students from minority ethnic communities. Both the focus group discussions and interviews were tape recorded.

The selection of institutions to participate in the case studies was influenced primarily by the findings of the national survey. From the analysis of the survey it was possible to identify a small number of institutions that appeared to be expressing a commitment towards preparing practitioners to work in a multi-ethnic society and were taking forward work in this area. In addition, as we were seeking to gain the views of newly qualified practitioners, it was important to approach institutions that had been offering the programmes for a sufficient length of time in order to ensure that there would be a pool of nurses and midwives who had completed the programmes and would be able to make informed comments on the extent to which they felt prepared to meet the needs of minority ethnic clients. The final criteria for identifying institutions was that they should be located in different parts of the country.

On the basis of the above criteria, three institutions were selected. Although it was not intended to be the case, they were all NHS colleges and were located in different regions of the country, in cities with a significant proportion of the local population drawn from different minority ethnic communities. In the first college we examined the midwifery programme, in the second both nursing and midwifery programmes and in the third the nursing programmes. Four focus group interviews per programme were undertaken comprising separate groups of students, teachers, newly qualified practitioners and mentors/assessors. Each focus group comprised an average of eight to ten volunteer participants. Individual interviews were undertaken with education and service managers in each of the sites. The number of interviews varied in each location on account of the different organizational structures. A total of 32 interviews were undertaken, 18 with education managers and 14 with service managers.

The core of the data presented in this chapter lies in the focus group interviews which were carried out in each location. However, in interpreting these data the researchers have benefited from the background information made available through the individual interviews with college and service managers. The focus groups have been subjected to two forms of analysis. The first was based upon identifying the major themes which were apparent in the discussion of the topics that structured the discussion. These themes were identified by two coders operating independently and were identified as phrases capturing the essence of the themes. Each focus group was thus reduced to a synoptic precis which was the sum of these phrases. These synopses were then analysed across the different focus groups.

The synopses of the focus group discussions have provided a basis for sketching the major characteristics of the learning experience in each case study location. Each case study will be briefly described and then the synoptic data will be presented. While some comments will inevitably be included in the presentation of these data, a fuller examination of the implications of this, and the subsequent content analysis, will be reserved for the chapters which follow. Consequently, we must ask the reader to accept that, while we have sought to present it in coherent elements, this is a chapter which is an accumulation of evidence, rather than a more literary presentation of an argument. That follows in the succeeding chapters.

After the synoptic analysis, the focus group data are examined through a finer filter in a content analysis approach which reveals continuities across the case studies, and some features of the branch and midwifery programmes are examined. These two modes of analysis, while carried out independently of each other, yield a comparable picture and together offer strong evidence regarding the current state of professional education in nursing and midwifery.

The first case study

The context

The first case study was of the midwifery programme offered by a large college of nursing and midwifery based in a city with a diversity of minority ethnic communities. Like all the other sites we would visit, the range of locations where placements would be offered included catchment areas that were very predominantly populated by the majority ethnic community. Thus placements, even in a city with areas of considerable minority ethnic community settlement, could not guarantee students an opportunity to work with a multi-ethnic clientele. Again like the other case study sites, the college had been through a process of institutional amalgamation and was in transition towards merging into higher education. Despite this experience, the research team found a very confident and cohesive management structure. Throughout the changes the head of the midwifery directorate had remained unchanged, and she and the head of pre-registration midwifery provided very clear professional leadership. The management style was one which was responsive to collective ownership of the programme. In the words of the head of midwifery, 'I like to see ideas coming up from the staff rather than going down. Very much that happens. We've got some people with some very good ideas' (1.2.10). This management style was very probably made much more effective by the relatively small size of the staff group and the very strong *esprit de corps* of staff and students as midwives. To the non-nursing qualified member of the research team this was a particularly striking aspect of the visits. The staff and students not only had a very strong collective identity as midwives; it was also pointedly defined in a sense of not being nurses. This is captured beautifully in this quotation:

> I came up through the nursing route and I know that there is a vast difference between the culture in nursing and midwifery. I also have a lot of experience of teaching direct entry midwives in the past and those that have gone through nursing and there's no doubt about it that they are very different to teach in every way. Because you shouldn't say that anybody has unlearning to do, because you don't unlearn, but if I can use that term, there is a lot of unlearning to do from the nurse that comes into midwifery. (1.22.10)

A further possible source of coherence on the programme is the apparent openness of communication between the educational setting and the practice placements. A midwifery manager in a large hospital confirmed the general management style by reporting that 'they've cascaded a sharing of a lot of the meetings right down the line, so not only senior midwives get involved or the heads' (1.5.10). More than that, she spoke warmly and positively of the links between the college and the seven different sites employed in providing practice placements. The picture painted was of fairly continuous open dialogue, and a relationship in which anxieties and particular interests would be openly declared and negotiated. This situation was summarized in these terms: 'When I did my training there were the educationalists and the clinical side and never the twain shall meet. You never used to see anybody except the clinical teachers as they were then. It is very different now. They feed off us and vice versa. And that's where the success has come from really' (1.5.9).

The closeness of this relationship is not completely replicated in the case of the link between the college and a further education college which provides much of the behavioural science input into the programme. Here again the personal relationships are warm and speak of mutual respect; but there is a greater autonomy between the two partners. In the words of a social science lecturer, 'We have a good relationship, but they don't tend to interfere much with what we do, and we don't interfere at all with what they do. But we do come together and work together for the times that we do meet' (1.6.8). This is much more of a pragmatically adequate relationship with necessary checks and balances in place: it is more of a cooperation than a full partnership. Anyone familiar with the politics of service teaching will find this state unremarkable. In fact, the degree of contact and mutual respect may be hard to match in many instances.

Thus, in moving on to examine the evidence emerging from the focus group discussions, we would suggest that the reader bears in mind this brief sketch of the context. It was a site which, for the research team, showed a spirited confidence in what they were collectively engaged in delivering. There was a scale of operation that facilitated contact among staff and a management style that seemed to maximize the coherence of a strong professional identity.

The synoptic analysis

The identification of ethnic diversity as an issue in the programme

As already noted, case study 1 has the good fortune to be based upon a relatively compact midwifery programme which, as will become apparent, made possible a good relationship, based on frequent interaction between staff and students, and a good relationship between the college-based staff and the mentors and assessors in practice. When asked to comment upon how the health care needs of minority ethnic clients were an issue in the programme, the students and teachers were both clear that it was explicitly incorporated into the curriculum. The students reported that cultural awareness was built into the first year of the curriculum, and that 'It's always cropping up.' Additionally, they identified formal lectures as an important input, complemented by, for example, lecturers sharing their own experience of working overseas. The midwifery practitioners, in reflecting upon their experience of the programme, particularly identified the sociology theme as a very significant input on issues relating to minority ethnic client needs. The teachers also identified the social science input as being important, but stressed that the curriculum was so structured that students were meeting clients within the first five weeks of the programme.

Both the teachers and the mentors observed that the college is situated in a city with a high proportion of minority ethnic residents, and that consequently this underpinned the importance of addressing ethnicity within the curriculum. Additionally, staff and students saw the opportunity of working with minority ethnic communities as a particularly valuable learning resource; and acknowledged that the demography of the city was such that this was not possible in all practice locations. The mentors and assessors discussed the fact that they felt that not enough was done to meet the needs of minority ethnic clients in all clinical contexts, and consequently it follows that the presence of minority clients does not guarantee an opportunity to observe good intercultural service delivery. Yet despite this the students felt that working with minority ethnic clients was a vital factor which kept ethnicity a continuous issue within their programme. In addition to the core curriculum, the teachers reported that special visits to minority ethnic community organizations and specific study days were employed to focus attention upon working in a multi-ethnic context.

The strengths of the educational programme
Many of the above themes re-emerged when the focus groups discussed the strengths of the programme. The students expressed considerable confidence in the competencies they had acquired to enable them to work with a multi-ethnic clientele. They felt that the classroom experience had given them a good grounding, and that in being encouraged to question they had been able to complement this knowledge through working with experienced midwives during practice. This situation was qualified by students' recognition of the hierarchy of power in the practice setting, for example, where they on occasions felt better informed than some current practitioners on ethnic-related issues and had to negotiate this within their student role. There was a sense of the students comparing themselves with qualified staff and feeling sufficiently confident of themselves as a vanguard of new practice to be able to share negative anecdotes about some 'older midwives'.

The teachers and mentors also identified the practice setting as a strength of the programme, with the mentors particularly valuing the experience of working with minority ethnic clients in a community-based placement, and somewhat derided 'doing ethnic minorities in the classroom'. It may also have been the case that for mentors pregnancy was an essential defining feature of any valuable experience, since visits to generic minority ethnic community centres were also discounted. The teachers, on the other hand, identified both of these activities as strengths within the programme. They also identified minority ethnic staff and students as a valuable resource within the programme, where their experience and knowledge was seen as making a distinctive contribution to majority ethnic students' learning.

Difficulties encountered and the limitations of the programme
Interestingly, when the focus groups moved on to discuss the difficulties encountered in training, the students expressed concern about the use of minority ethnic staff in their placements. They felt that too often they were used as interpreters for other staff, and consequently taken away from their own duties; and that additionally colleagues tended to assume that they could be consulted as experts in relation to all ethnic-related matters. In fact, not for the only time, language was reported as a difficulty, with students and practitioners seeing language barriers as an impediment to good practice. Both these focus groups were critical of existing interpretation services. Indeed, the teachers reflected upon the current Eurocentric nature of service design and delivery, and suggested that the more familiar students became with the practice areas, the more they came to identify deficiencies in the provision for minority ethnic clients. While this may be an analytic virtue, it also impacts upon the opportunity to observe good practice. In fact this is likely to be further exacerbated, as the teachers noted, by the fact that trust catchment boundaries impinged upon the construction of students' placement opportunities. Consequently, students certainly could not be guaranteed the opportunity of working with minority ethnic clients.

The students identified further potential difficulties with practice placements, including the racist behaviour of some qualified midwives, which obstructed students in their attempts to put their acquired cross-cultural knowledge into practice. And echoing the teachers' earlier comment, the students in their discussion also noted that the lack of resources in hospitals to meet the health care needs of minority ethnic clients defined part of their learning experience. The students also had an analytic understanding of the interaction of class and 'race', and their expression in the 'inverse care law' which informed their understanding of this situation.

The difficulty of integrating theory with practice was raised in different ways within the focus groups. The teachers observed that they were dependent on the mentors for feedback upon students' clinical progress, yet in some instances their work with minority ethnic clients may not be assessed at all. Mentors felt that the timing of community placements within the programme did not allow sufficient opportunity for students to have a continuous and coherent experience of practice. The students, on the other hand, reported something of their difficulties in translating cultural awareness from theory into practice. For example, they reported difficulties in reality in accepting differing cultural norms as experienced with some of their clients, and observed that it is not possible to be taught in the classroom how to deal with ambivalent feelings towards clients. As midwives and women, some reported, for example, that they felt anger and distress when caring for a woman who has been circumcised. This was an example which recurred when the practitioners discussed their similar experiences of having to negotiate a mismatch between their personal values and those of a minority ethnic client.

Moving on to discuss their perceptions of the limitations in professional programmes the teachers, mentors and practitioners all identified aspects of the mismatch between the time and resources available and the extensive demands of addressing the issue adequately. The mentors, for example, noted the great diversity of minority ethnic communities in their area and consequently the impossibility of addressing the range of cultural knowledge required adequately. The teachers complemented this anxiety in their discussion of the number of topics that needed to be included in the curriculum and of the consequent pressure of time when they were trying to plan programmes. A variant of this concern was shared by students, teachers and practitioners, who in their discussions returned to the variable amount of time students may have available to experience working with minority ethnic clients; one of the factors impinging upon this included resistance from the trust hospitals to students moving across trust boundaries, thus limiting the diversity of experience any particular student might have. And students and practitioners noted the time constraints in the practice setting, which set limits on the time that could be spent with minority ethnic clients, with a consequent impact upon the quality of learning and of care. Additionally, the teachers and mentors recognized in their discussions the limitations of their own developing knowledge of intercultural care as a factor in shaping the students' learning. And both students and practitioners reported on the negative consequences of the cross-cultural ignorance and hostile attitudes of some existing practitioners in contributing to a culture in the workplace which inhibited students' learning.

How the programme might be developed
Practice placements emerged as a focus of attention when the groups discussed how professional education might usefully be developed. Both the practitioners and mentors were concerned to advocate a more systematic regulation of practice placements, so that the opportunity of working with a multi-ethnic clientele and of contact with a diversity of minority ethnic communities may be guaranteed. As an adjunct to this proposal, the students argued that there was a need to improve the transcultural skills of qualified midwives, as this would not only improve the care of clients but would also significantly improve their learning environment. The students and practitioners saw a need more actively to bring the user's voice into

the college through a policy of bringing in invited lecturers. They both saw a need to recruit more minority ethnic students.

The teachers had an extensive discussion about how they might improve their own competencies to prepare students for working in a multi-ethnic context. Among a variety of strategies, they argued for a need initially to have a more developed knowledge of the range of competencies and experience distributed among the staff group, so that they might more efficiently be fed into the curriculum. They also advocated the use of refresher courses and post-registration education to facilitate the acquisition of new skills. The teachers were confident in their sharing in a 'dynamic curriculum' which was responsive to new challenges and capable of change. In this context, they were open about their ability to learn from the students' experience through reading and marking their work and through discussions with them.

The adequacy of respondents' own preparation to work with minority ethnic clients
This willingness to be reflexive is also apparent in the teachers' discussion of the adequacy of their own preparation to meet the needs of a multi-ethnic clientele. Interestingly, although the teachers reported feeling inadequately equipped to teach and support students in this area, they had none the less been successful in instilling a sense of competence in their students. Both the current students and the practitioners, as past students, felt that while there was still much to learn, they had been well prepared to begin practice with a multi-ethnic clientele. The students, for example, spoke of having been taught to take a holistic approach to care, and that therefore difference and individuality could be incorporated within this framework. They felt that they had been given a foundation of skills that were capable of being re-addressed and built upon. It was noticeable that they saw minority ethnic clients themselves as an important continued source for new learning. Both the students and practitioners, however, saw linguistic barriers as a continuing disadvantage to their ability to give appropriate care to all clients.

The adequacy of the preparation of practitioners in general
The students and practitioners were not so generous in their appraisal of the adequacy of preparation of practitioners in general. There was a general view that the older generation of midwives were typically only superficially equipped to meet the needs of minority ethnic clients, with some proportion being positively hostile to addressing the needs of these clients. The teachers, while identifying the many variables which might determine a midwife's current competence, also echoed this view. Among the students there was a clear sense in which they saw themselves as a new generation of practitioners who have benefited from a more extensive life experience of living in a multi-ethnic society, and from a more multicultural relevant education, than their predecessors.

Concluding the first case study

This synoptic analysis presents a picture of professional education which is consistent with the research teams' experience in the college, and with their individual interviews with senior staff and others. This analysis presents a picture of the issue of working with minority ethnic clients being permeated throughout the learning environment. The opportunity to work with minority ethnic clients is very highly valued and consequently the happenstance nature of encountering this experience is raised as a concern. It should be said, however, that both college managers and a midwifery manager in a large hospital were clearly aware of this and spoke of trying to ensure a diversity of experience. However, other factors also impinged upon the quality of the practice placement, not least among which was the inadequate competence of many existing practitioners in working with a multi-ethnic clientele, and the hostility and racism towards minority ethnic clients which scarred the working culture. Importantly, there is also an explicit recognition of the personal ambiguity that may be experienced in the attempt to work with an acceptance of another culture's mores. Language emerges as a major difficulty in work with specific minority ethnic clients; and, while minority ethnic practitioners are specifically valued for their contribution to nursing provision in a multi-ethnic context, the students express some anxiety at the abuse of such colleagues in their use as interpreters. All these broad issues will re-emerge in the successive case studies. What is perhaps distinctive here is the strength of the conviction held by these midwifery students that they have been equipped to begin practice in a multi-ethnic context.

The second case study

The context

The second case study was based in a large college of nursing and midwifery located in a city with a considerable 'Asian' population and a diversity of other smaller minority ethnic communities. It had already merged with a school of midwifery and was shortly to merge yet again with a higher education institution. There had been a rationalization (shedding) of staff in the college and this had been countered by an active policy of developing a bank of casual, part-time or occasional contributors who helped to sustain the programme of formal teaching. The college offered a complete portfolio of pre-registration programmes as well as a full post-registration programme. The management of the college in interviews indicated that a willingness to address the preparation of practitioners to work in a multi-ethnic context had been driven by a number of factors. These were: the demography of the local area, which made ethnic diversity a self-evident reality; the responsiveness and initiative of staff who recognized this as a feature of contemporary practice, and wished to develop an appropriate professional response; and external pressure from trusts and 'the Region', which had reflected Health of the Nation priorities in indicating competencies in intercultural practice as part of the professional repertoire to be expected of practitioners entering the professions. This is an account which also emerged from our interviews with respondents in the other case studies. In these instances the comments identify sources of influence for change; but they do not adequately provide the basis for weighting their relative significance. We could, however, observe that our national questionnaire data (Chapter 4) demonstrate that colleges may ignore this issue with impunity. And these case studies indicate variations in coherent commitment between, and within, institutions that have claimed to have embraced transcultural competence as an educational task. In this case study, for example, the common foundation programme leader identified the fact that an estimated '25–30 per cent of the teachers are from ethnic [sic] backgrounds' (2.4.1) as being a particular factor in enabling this college to be able to develop a competence in preparing students for working in a multi-ethnic context.

In comparison to the small and cohesive structure of the first case study, case study 2 is much larger, and has more organizational opportunities for staff to fragment. For example, a senior manager in the college reports that while there are curriculum leaders with administrative responsibility to deliver the teaching in, say, social sciences, biological sciences, nursing studies and midwifery studies, there are no equivalent programme teams. The curriculum leaders identify their resource needs and bring these together from a pool of people with appropriate expertise. These may include staff from the about to be merged higher education institution or staff from trusts and elsewhere. It is a more diverse institutional structure than in the first case study, and collective identities may be more diffuse. Personal tutors in the common foundation programme, for example, offer support to all students irrespective of their future trajectory.

This diversity within the institution has a consequent parallel in the very wide range of agencies providing placements over a very considerable area, spanning city, suburban and rural settings. One positive feature of this is the diversity of experience available to students. However, the management staff interviewed in college and in clinical settings were also very aware that the demographic distribution of minority ethnic communities meant that they occurred as a significant client population in some locations and not in others. The college senior management had sought to ensure that all the students had experience of a variety of placements; and hence they were all likely to have the experience of working with minority ethnic clients at some point in their programmes. But this was acknowledged as being a very imperfect situation, and was illustrated by the mental health director, who identified a particular concern:

I guess the imbalance of exposure that people may get. That people will have the opportunity to work with people from specific cultures depending on who is admitted or who is in the clinical areas at the time. We haven't got a way of controlling and saying that people are getting a fair spread of different cultures; and experience with people with differing mental health problems with people with different cultures . . . It would be unrealistic to try and rearrange the programme and make sure that everybody got a spread. (2.3.7)

A further organizational consequence of this plethora of placements lay in the difficulty of ensuring efficient liaison between the college staff and personnel in the clinical settings. The research team became aware of this as an issue through interviews with individual managers in the service agencies. It was not that there was an obvious breakdown of communication, or a crisis of confidence in the relation between the partners in the education process. Rather, it was more a recurrent sense of a gentle territorial *cordon sanitaire* between them: a boundary which was sufficiently permeable to allow for essential communication, sufficient to keep the parts in touch with the whole; but a boundary that left a good deal unexplored. For example, a senior nurse in a large hospital, on being asked whether she had a feel for what was happening on the pre-registration programme in terms of addressing students' ability to work in a multi-ethnic context, typified by a hospital such as hers, replied: 'No I haven't.' She followed this by reporting that they had recently established an operational working group with the college, which would meet quarterly, but went on to conclude that 'We haven't had a system of regular communication' (2.12.10). A rather similar response was obtained from a mental health manager for a large hospital trust, who indicated that he felt that they did not have a good relationship with the college; and suggested that the trust was at least partially culpable. 'I don't think we, as a trust, actually communicate properly, and I think that's partly due to the size and way that it's managed. We have a lot of communication problems' (2.2.9). A clinical nurse specialist in a large hospital identified one form of ensuring a linkage between the college and practice as failing. Specifically, she was highly critical of the adequacy of the preparation of mentors, and was clear that the current preparation of mentors was inadequate, with too much trivialized by presentation to mentors in much too short a time. Given the strong critique of the transcultural competence of the mentors coming from the students in these case studies, this practitioner's subsequent suggestion was more than appropriate:

I think maybe that's a way that they could improve things by saying, 'OK, well look, what are the things that we're teaching our P2000 students which the mentors won't have had access to.' And then using that opportunity to update staff and then potentially you would reduce the theory and practice gap, because there's always going to be a gap if the people who are mentoring don't know or haven't covered the same ground as the students. (2.1.13)

This need not be a one-way transfer of expertise, for the research team also identified within the local trusts pockets of initiative in developing services for minority ethnic communities of which college staff were sometimes ignorant. For trusts to insert their ideas of new practice into the college's curriculum might, on occasions, be a valuable route to harmonizing practice and promoting a change in practice culture.

The synoptic analysis

The identification of ethnic diversity as an issue in the programmes

Something of the power of demography was suggested through the focus group discussions in the second case study. Discussing how the health care needs of minority ethnic communities were made an issue within the education, all the student groups and the adult branch mentors made a point of saying that living in that city made it an unavoidable issue. This demography was also seen as having significant implications, in that many of the practice settings allowed students to have experience of working with minority ethnic clients. That this was so lent credibility to the widespread expression of the opinion that the needs of minority ethnic clients were highlighted throughout the taught curriculum and in the practice settings. Midwifery students, mental health branch teachers and adult branch teachers and students all supported this view; yet in apparent contradiction the midwifery practitioners, adult and mental health practitioners all suggested that this had not been their experience of the programmes, with the placements and the social science input being identified as the core site of relevant input. The probable answer seems to lie in the fact that the ethos and content of the college may have changed; since, for example, the midwifery teachers reported that it used to be part of the hidden curriculum, but is now permeated throughout the curriculum. Since all the students saw themselves benefiting from living in a multi-ethnic city, it is perhaps appropriate that they are identified by the midwifery and mental health branch practitioners and the adult branch teachers as having a significant input into programmes through bringing ethnic issues into discussions within the learning environment. Additionally, the mental health branch students valued the large number of minority ethnic staff who were able to incorporate their own experience into their teaching.

The strengths of the programmes

The presence of minority ethnic staff was identified by the mental health branch students and the midwifery students as one of the strengths of their programme. The greatest consensus in discussions of the strength of the programme was in an appreciation of the variety of practice settings, which enabled students to experience working with minority ethnic clients. The adult branch students' discussion provided illumination of this theme by identifying the practice placement as the location where the general awareness and cross-cultural input of the taught programme can be put into practice, and be developed at greater depth. They noted how much they benefited from the support of clients' families in coming to develop these skills. Thus all the students had a sense that the programme raised their awareness of ethnic issues in practice through its recurrence in their programme, and they valued specific inputs which introduced cross-cultural knowledge. The placements that they obtained were, however, critical in enabling them to build upon this foundation. The possibility of consolidating this integration of theory and practice was also seen as being promoted by the creation of a context in which students were encouraged to discuss issues with staff; and this aspect of the learning environment was in differing ways identified by the adult branch, midwifery and mental health branch teachers as a strength of the programme.

Difficulties encountered and the limitations of the programmes
If the focus groups were confident in identifying strengths in their programme they were equally forthcoming in qualifying this view through their discussions of the difficulties they felt were experienced in relation to it addressing the preparation of practitioners to work with a multi-ethnic clientele. Language once more surfaced as a near universal problem in delivering appropriate care, and was identified as an enduring difficulty in seeking to work with minority ethnic clients. Among the teaching staff, their own lack of competence was raised by the midwifery mentors and practitioners, the mental health branch practitioners and the adult branch practitioners and teachers as a significant difficulty. The midwifery and adult branch practitioners, as well as the midwifery mentors, raised in their discussions the difficulties which practitioners may experience in handling personal reactions to other cultural norms. These comments perhaps provide some justification for the sentiments shared by the midwifery and adult branch students that not all mentors are equipped to offer support in the acquisition of transcultural skills. Indeed there was a sub-text in which some of the students felt that they were educating the mentors. Additionally, the adult and mental health branch students commented upon the hostility towards minority ethnic clients which they encountered while on their placements. Further difficulties with the practice context were discussed by the adult and mental health branch teachers, who saw the health care system as in various ways being dominated by majority values and models of health, which impinged upon both patient care and the learning environment of students. Given the value attached to placements as a positive contribution to the students' learning, it is not surprising that the happenstance nature of the allocation and availability of relevant placements was raised as a problem by midwifery students, adult branch practitioners and mental health teachers.

The more general concerns expressed around the limitations of the programme in addressing the needs of minority ethnic clients were diverse, with only a few themes having a broad visibility. Language again emerged with near universal recognition of its having a deleterious impact upon both practice and learning, while the inadequacy of current practitioners to act as appropriate role models and mentors was also heavily stressed by the adult branch practitioners, mentors and students and by midwifery practitioners and mental health branch students. One novel concern worth noting was expressed by the adult branch teachers, who felt there was a possible anxiety attached to attempts to ensure the availability of placements with minority ethnic clients: this took the form of a concern that they might be accused of setting up an 'ethnic minority peep show'. The question of the legitimate access to the experience of minority ethnic clients is one which has been touched upon earlier, and is certainly something which requires attention as programmes seek to 'tap into the community'.

How the programmes might be developed

Language reappears as an area where in future developments in professional education, the opportunity to acquire even a basic facility in minority community languages would be valued; both mental health branch students and practitioners, and midwifery students and practitioners advocated such training. The staff groups addressed current deficits in advocating more extensive preparation in transcultural knowledge, with adult branch and midwifery practitioners and mentors and the mental health branch teachers all agreeing upon this as a necessity. One possible contribution to meeting this demand offered by the mental health and adult branch practitioners and the adult mentors and mental health branch teachers was that programmes should have closer links with the minority ethnic communities and have more input from their members into the curriculum. Two groups in their discussion picked up an aspect of structural ethnicity, in that the mental health branch students and the adult branch practitioners both went beyond promoting cultural awareness to assert that practitioners needed additionally to be taught how to identify where the resources lay in the minority ethnic communities that could be linked to service delivery. This was a valuable reminder that cultural awareness training may have the dangerous capacity to promote a view of ethnicity as the cultural property of individuals and fail to address its structural characteristics.

The adequacy of respondents' own preparation to work with minority ethnic clients

In discussing their own sense of adequacy to work in an ethnically sensitive way with a multi-ethnic clientele, the very great majority of the staff groups (adult branch teachers, practitioners, mentors, mental health branch teachers and practitioners and the midwifery teachers) reported that they had not been adequately prepared through their own professional education, although some spoke of compensating for this through self-directed learning through their practice. The adult branch and midwifery students were more confident that their current education had given them the basis to start practising in a multi-ethnic context. Even the more reticent view of the mental health branch students that they did not feel sufficiently prepared was qualified by their assertion that they were still better equipped than a lot of qualified staff. An interesting qualification of the adult branch students' self-confidence came in their discussion of the fact that their experience had been predominantly with 'Asian' clients. This must be a likely consequence of the geographical location of all programmes, where local demography will have a strong impact upon the minority ethnic communities which become the focus of transcultural concern within the curriculum.

The adequacy of preparation of practitioners in general

Perhaps not surprisingly, given the views expressed earlier in these focus groups, when they came to discuss the adequacy of preparation of practitioners in general to work with a multi-ethnic clientele, the dominant view was negative. While in all the discussions there was an acceptance of individual variability, including the adult branch practitioners offering the faint praise that on the whole practitioners were more aware of the issues than previously, there was a general consensus that the level of preparation was inadequate. Some comments were extremely harsh. Perhaps the nursing practitioners could have taken heart from the judgement offered in the adult branch students' discussion that it was the doctors who were the least well prepared to work with minority ethnic clients.

Concluding the second case study

This synoptic analysis presents a picture of an institution which has made the preparation of practitioners to work with minority ethnic communities an evident concern. Students and staff are aware that it is permeated throughout the programme. The happenstance nature of placements again emerges as a concern for staff and students; and the inadequate competence of many mentors and current practitioners to work in a multi-ethnic context is again identified as a significant problem. Racism and hostility in the practice placement are confirmed as presenting a problem. Language difficulties are again a visible problem in the delivery of appropriate health care.

This case study, more than the first, makes visible the importance of the quality of communication between the college and practice settings. There is evidence here of this being inadequate to maximize the quality of shared learning, rather than of it having broken down sufficiently to cause a crisis in training. But the implication remains that the system works despite the quality of routine communication rather than because of it. This case study also pointed out how local demography may determine the minority ethnic communities that become incorporated into education programmes, with potential consequences for geographically mobile students. And it illustrated how cultural awareness training may fail to identify the structural resources of local minority ethnic communities.

The third case study

The context

The third case study was of a large multi-site college located in a large city with a considerable and varied minority ethnic population. Within the past 18 months there had been very real stress as it had modularized its programme, and it was currently contemplating merger into higher education. Unlike that of case study 1, this institution had a much more top-down management style and the research team were struck by the sense of detachment from the institution they felt among the staff.

In this case study the senior management had set up a project to look at equal opportunities in the curriculum. In the words of a senior manager, 'I have to say it wasn't very successful because it ended up really being a crusade for equal opportunities between men and women' (3.9.10). This initiative had itself been put in place because a group established to look at equal opportunities had 'basically never met', a fact which was interpreted as perhaps 'a reflection on the priority that people gave it' (3.9.10). Following this experience, the college had now identified a key group of people within the staff who would teach issues related to 'ethnic minorities and equal opportunities in the curriculum'. These people had been given training by external consultants brought in for the purpose. The intention was that the group would then cascade knowledge on to other staff. Interestingly, the focus of this group was not to explore the development of curricular content, but to address how staff should address topics of ethnic diversity and challenge oppressive behaviour. This was an imaginative initiative but not one whose impact was detected in the research team's interviews and focus group discussions. Perhaps it was too early in the development of this policy.

This college had adopted an explicit equal opportunities policy in relation to recruitment and at the time of the data collection was initiating a systematic research review of its recruitment practices. However, despite the evidence of management's acknowledgement of equal opportunities issues in relation to ethnic diversity, the case study provided the least persuasive evidence of meeting the needs of minority ethnic communities being permeated throughout the curriculum. The data from the students presented below, for example, indicated that while they felt that ethnicity and care in a multi-ethnic context was specifically raised in the common foundation programme, and particularly within the sociology input, it was not sustained with equal emphasis in the branch programmes. Of the three case studies, this one demonstrated the least apparent coherence in planning for the preparation of students to work with a multi-ethnic clientele.

Possibly one answer came from the multi-site nature of the institution and the internal organization of the teaching staff. Thus, for example, a senior manager for the common foundation programme offered this insight:

the thing that occurs to me most strongly is that the way the college is, I really shouldn't say divided, it's organized into departments – I think divided is a more appropriate word – then different themes within this programme are dealt with by different departments. So the nursing department doesn't handle the sociology, for example; and psychology comes from a different department. I think probably most of the formal work on the issues that you're interested in actually lie within a different department. (3.11.2)

Later, this same respondent indicated that 'considering the programme is nursing, the Department of Nursing Education is a very small department' (3.11.3).

In a modularized structure it is quite possible that this pattern of departmental structures, with the relative autonomy that often goes with it, militates against the development of a smooth linkage between elements in a shared curriculum. This may be particularly so on a multi-site programme. Additionally, however, this programme had a strong emphasis on students' self-directed learning, which may further have loosened the guaranteed coherence of the curriculum. Not only did students seem to have significant degrees of educational freedom, staff also seemed, in relation to addressing the health care needs of minority ethnic clients, to be able to opt in or out. This was perhaps most unambiguously declared in an individual interview:

> *Interviewer*: In an ideal world, what would you see yourself wanting to do in terms of developing the programme in relation to the needs of ethnic minority clients? Is there a range of possibilities that are imaginable?
>
> *Respondent*: I would say first of all I think that everybody's got their interests, everybody's got an axe to grind and I think this particular topic isn't one of them. It's not one of the things that I want to get up and shout to the world about. If you want to talk about ethics then I'll be up there with the best of them. So it's not something that I've got a burning desire to take forward personally; though I've several colleagues who have and I think that's good. Fortunately we don't all try to be experts at everything. (3.11.14)

This response sees addressing the health care needs of minority ethnic clients as one special interest among many. Although the respondent goes on to indicate that ethnicity does crop up in lectures, there is a resistance to addressing ethnicity as a major variable in health care. There is instead a preference for an individualist interpretation of a holistic approach. 'I personally prefer to see the whole topic as a matter of everybody's different, everybody's got individual needs' (3.11.14). While this member of the college staff had been inclined to let others take forward multi-ethnic issues, a colleague who had sought to do just that reported a feeling that the initiative had not been supported by more senior management.

Case Study 3 was characterized by a sense that the institution had undergone very significant managerial and pedagogic changes. While equal opportunity issues were high on the management agenda, a commitment to developing an education experience that would equip students to work in a multi-ethnic context was much more elusive within the institution. Importantly, the college staff appeared to lack a sense of their collective endeavour.

The synoptic analysis

The identification of ethnic diversity as an issue in the programmes

When we looked at how the health care needs of minority ethnic communities were made an issue within the curriculum in the third location, in a variety of ways it was made apparent that this did figure in the curriculum. However, while it was accepted by all the categories of respondents that it was present in the curriculum, a number of qualifying comments emerged. Both the adult branch students and adult branch practitioners observed that it was not made a big issue. Although the mental health branch students agreed that it was addressed in a general fashion in the common foundation programme, they also commented that it only became an issue when working in placements with minority ethnic clients; a comment echoed by the adult branch students. The view which had the widest consensus across the focus groups was that the geographical location of the institution, with the attendant demography including large minority ethnic communities, had made the needs of these distinct client groups a matter for concern. Within the adult branch, the teachers, students and practitioners shared a belief that the students were self-directed and played an important role in bringing issues of ethnicity into the programme through discussions in seminars and in sessions where students were feeding back their clinical experience.

The strengths of the programmes

When we looked at how the topic 'strengths of the programme' was discussed in the focus groups, the synopses revealed that the space for self-directed learning was a highly valued aspect of the programme structure, with the mental health branch students, mental health branch teachers and adult branch students particularly identifying this as a virtue. Additionally, there was a widespread recognition in both the adult and mental health branch programmes that the programme provided an introduction to specific elements of transcultural knowledge through taught inputs. The fact that assignments expected an integration of ethnicity as an issue was regarded as useful for focusing attention upon minority ethnic community health needs. The holistic ethos of contemporary nursing emerged as a clear feature of the adult branch programme, where teachers, students and mentors all invoked holism as a vehicle for opening up issues relevant to working in a multi-ethnic context. Among the adult branch practitioners there was a retrospective appreciation of the valuable learning opportunities which had been made possible through community and clinical experience.

Difficulties encountered and the limitations of the programmes
Interestingly, the focus group discussion of the difficulties experienced with the programme was more extensive than that of its strengths. A range of comments addressed the general problem of ensuring an integrated coherence in weaving ethnicity-related issues into the curriculum. The adult and mental health branch students as well as their teachers all commented on the fact that 'race' and ethnicity was not a common theme throughout the programme. Mental health branch students in particular were concerned that the clinical placements did not all reflect the ethnic diversity of the city, and that an additional problem was to be found in the random allocation of placements. These factors could be generalized to all students and resulted in the fact that students could not be required to work with minority ethnic clients; nor could individual students be guaranteed the opportunity for such experience. In fact, one of the difficulties that emerged related to the inadequacy of resources to provide adequate health care provision for minority ethnic clients in the clinical settings, and to the racism found among the staff in this context. Adult branch students and mentors and mental health branch teachers all commented upon the racism that was to be found in the clinical settings. Nor could it be assumed that this was a problem only to be encountered outside the college; for both mental health branch teachers and adult branch teachers discussed the difficulties they experienced when faced with students' resistance to the introduction of topics to do with racism or minority ethnic community health needs on to the programme.

This attitudinal resistance to addressing the needs of the minority ethnic communities was compounded by an emerging consensus across the focus groups that there was, in addition to the already noted inadequate resources for minority ethnic clients, an inadequate available range of transcultural competence among the nursing staff. Thus the clinical setting emerges as being far from an ideal learning environment. The adult branch practitioners talked openly about their own sense of inadequacy in relation to their ignorance of specific transcultural knowledge and lack of competence to address the needs of minority ethnic clients. The general lack of personal and institutional accommodation to the reality of having a multi-ethnic clientele was illustrated by the frequency with which language was identified as a major difficulty in the clinical context. All the adult branch focus groups raised this as an issue and identified the specific difficulties as arising in the lack of adequate interpreting services and the barrier to communication which mutual incomprehension constituted. Additionally, echoing the negative attitudes and racism identified already, inappropriate language had been observed to be used by staff towards both clients and students from minority ethnic communities. It is against this context of the failure of the majority ethnic communities' construction and delivery of nursing care that expectations of the role of minority ethnic personnel should perhaps be located. Both adult branch students and teachers regretted the relative absence of minority ethnic staff in the college and in the clinical settings. The teachers in particular were concerned that there should be such people in senior positions to provide role models for minority ethnic students. The mental health students similarly expressed concern that recruitment did not in their view succeed in attracting students from minority ethnic communities.

Given this extensive concern about the difficulties encountered in professional education, irrespective of the branch being followed, it is perhaps not surprising that there was also an expressed anxiety about the difficulties of integrating theory and practice. Since both the taught programme and the practice setting were found wanting, it is hardly surprising that the students should have found this famously difficult equation awkward to resolve in this context.

When they were discussing current limitations in education and practice, there was an indication among staff of a concern with the adequacy of their current knowledge of issues related to health care provision for minority ethnic communities. Adult branch practitioners spoke of their feelings of inadequacy in this area, and mental health branch teachers identified a need for staff development and training to enable them to feel comfortable in addressing these issues. They also expressed a concern that the curriculum did not adequately reflect the multi-ethnic client population in Britain, and felt a need for guidelines about how such issues should be addressed. At the same time these teachers noted the current pressure on the curriculum and the consequent time limitation when there were so many competing priorities. From the point of view of the students' opportunity to gain experience of working with minority ethnic clients, both adult branch teachers and students bewailed the lack of systematic organization of placements, such that students were not guaranteed a diversity of placements. This might be a particularly important consideration given the feedback about the attitudinal environment in placements. Mental health branch teachers spoke of the NHS as being a white establishment and adult branch students spoke of some staff in placements as being racist.

Concern with the learning environment in placements was also expressed in relation to the current poor response of hospitals to the needs of minority ethnic clients, with both adult branch mentors and practitioners raising this as an issue. Both of these groups, along with the mental health branch students, identified language and inadequate interpretation services as a specific problem. The mental health branch teachers saw this current state of the NHS as a factor affecting the recruitment of minority ethnic students; a situation they lamented as undesirable.

How the programmes might be developed
In the third case study there was no shortage of suggestions for further developments which might improve professional education. There was widespread agreement that the opportunity to work with minority ethnic clients was central: mental health and adult branch students, as well as adult branch teachers, mentors and practitioners, all made this point. As well as a more structured regulation of practice placements to facilitate this possibility, additional suggestions included ghosting practitioners who had regular contact with minority ethnic clients, and arranging visits to enable students to experience minority cultures *in situ*. Adult branch students and practitioners felt that there was a need to bring minority ethnic community experiences into the programme by inviting users and community members to contribute to the learning experience. There was a need felt for a greater degree of planning in the integration of transcultural issues into the curriculum, with mental health branch students and adult branch teachers particularly explicit in seeking a clearer framework that would inform the continuity of relevant inputs throughout the programme. Adult branch students and practitioners also advocated more cultural awareness training being integrated into the curriculum.

Following upon the concerns expressed earlier about racism in the practice context, it was appropriate that this was identified as an area which needed to be addressed in any future developments in professional education. Mental health branch teachers specifically recommended that racism in health care should be given greater visibility within the curriculum, and that resistance, anger and denial in discussions of ethnicity and racism in the classroom needed to be addressed. Adult branch students also pursued this issue, and argued that students needed to be enabled to analyse their own perceptions of racism, and that practitioners should be taught how to deal with racism in the practice setting. Yet again, the necessity of recruiting nurses from minority ethnic communities was identified as an issue, with mental health branch students and teachers urging this as a necessary priority.

The interests of particular respondents in looking at possible future developments were apparent in the mental health branch students' perception that the common foundation programme was too general in its approach and they wished for it to have a closer fit with the professional concerns of the mental health branch programme. However, they also recognized that at present it was the common foundation programme which contributed most to their understanding of ethnicity and transcultural practice and they wished that agenda to be more adequately carried through into the mental health branch curriculum. Teachers and mentors, on the other hand, had concerns specific to their own location in the education process, and adult branch mentors felt that they were not sufficiently informed about the curriculum, while adult branch teachers wished for more feedback from the students in order to produce a more coherent learning experience. The adult branch teachers and mentors also identified a need for further professional development and suggested that there was a need for study days and post-registration programmes on culture, 'race' and ethnicity to facilitate the acquisition of relevant skills.

The adequacy of respondents' own preparation to work with multi-ethnic clients

When asked to reflect upon the adequacy of their own preparation to work with minority ethnic clients, the respondents in the third case study were somewhat pessimistic. Responses ranged from an open declaration of not feeling adequately prepared, to discussions around a felt need for more basic understanding of issues prior to being able to begin to feel more competent. The adult branch practitioners, mental health and adult branch teachers focus groups all expressed some sense of not being adequately prepared. Students, on the other hand, were more likely to declare a sense of some basic competence and to reflect upon how they had acquired it. Both the adult branch and the mental health branch students emphasized the role of self-directed personal learning, with a related discounting of the relevance of the formal programme input. Interestingly, and perhaps less surprisingly, the staff echoed the importance of personal experience in building up their own knowledge base. Mental health branch teachers and adult branch mentors and teachers all asserted the importance of such life experience, with the adult branch practitioners additionally noting that much depended upon the opportunities one had had for relevant experience in practice placements as a student.

The adequacy of the preparation of practitioners in general

When asked to comment upon the adequacy of current practitioners in general, all the focus groups provided a much less reticent response, with the adult branch teachers, practitioners and students and the mental health branch teachers and students offering up a variety of negative responses. There was a widespread feeling that practitioners were far from adequately prepared to work with a multi-ethnic clientele; although there were some interesting qualifications to this. Both adult branch students and mentors felt that one's competence would depend upon where one trained, and the adult branch practitioners were of the opinion that at least nursing and midwifery practitioners were better prepared in this area than doctors. Reflecting a positive sense of group identity, the adult branch students felt that things would improve as more Project 2000 students entered into practice. Equally, they felt that improvements would follow from more minority ethnic students moving into the field.

Concluding the third case study

The major themes identified in the previous two case studies are again to be found here. The happenstance nature of placements is here more chronically evident than in the prior two. The inadequate competence of many existing practitioners to act as role models in caring for minority ethnic clients was again confirmed, as was the existence of racial hostility in the practice setting. The value of practitioners and teachers from minority ethnic communities as an important education and practice resource was also reasserted.

In this case study there was less evidence of an awareness of ethnic diversity being consistently permeated throughout the curriculum. The programme structure allowed for considerable autonomy for staff and students. Consequently, within the curriculum staff had a considerable degree of autonomy over how they chose to prioritize issues within their teaching. Equally, the students are encouraged to be self-directed and active in their learning. The research teams' interim conclusion, subsequently agreed by the college staff, was that these two forms of autonomy meant that there was no evident continuity of issues of ethnicity and practice in a multicultural context being presented as an ongoing and necessary aspect of professional competence. Indeed, for some students such issues could be peripheralized by their cumulative exercise of choice. The research team additionally fed back to the college a perception that in their institution modularization and the existing management structure had had negative consequences. Specifically, in the feedback it was suggested that 'This structure produces a sort of sense in which members of staff can easily begin to see themselves almost as contractual employees – "I do that, I do it well, what's your problem?" – as opposed to having a sense of being part of a coherent entity' (3.14.12). This was agreed as a reasonable reading of the situation. Consequently, it would seem that this case study has pointedly identified another significant variable in determining institutions' responses to providing a learning environment that will prepare students for working in a multi-ethnic context. Simply stated, the curriculum cannot be seen as being independent of the institutional structure and management style. The researchers tentatively suggested that in this institution the practical demands of administering a modular system within the existing structures made it difficult for middle management staff to provide professional leadership in terms of shaping the content of the curriculum. Their tasks have become more administrative than innovative.

The third case study provided an opportunity to observe a large institution managing change under circumstances of real pressure. The staff were committed to their students and their profession, yet collectively there were barriers to developing a coherent response to meeting the need to prepare students for working with a multi-ethnic clientele.

This analysis of the case studies has thus far examined each institution separately. In order to reveal the interrelation of factors within a single organizational context, in the following section we provide an analysis of the data which reveals continuities across institutional boundaries.

The content analysis

As previously explained, in addition to the analysis of each case study separately, a further strategy was adopted to ensure that common features of the data which applied across programmes and case study sites could be identified. The taped interviews were subsequently re-analysed from the perspective of emerging themes identified within the synoptic analysis. Through this process a broader set of categories was generated, which became the structure for a coding frame through which the interviews could be content analysed. Content analysis was carried out by three independent coders, who achieved an inter-rater reliability score of 86.5 per cent. It is useful to compare the results of the two analyses as, despite the diverse nature of the case study centres, and their wide geographical separation, their shared concerns become clearer. Furthermore, it is possible to identify issues which are attributable to one particular programme across different institutions. This is important in determining strategies which may have been successfully employed to overcome potential barriers to supporting students to function effectively with a multi-ethnic clientele.

Practice experience

The nature of the practice experience stands out as having a major determining effect on the students' learning opportunities, and in consequence upon their acquisition of skills in transcultural competence. There is common agreement among students, teachers, practitioners and mentors/assessors across programmes and case study centres that practice placements cannot guarantee contact with minority ethnic clients. Three out of the four focus groups in case study 1, eight out of 12 in case study 2 and five out of eight in case study 3 reported this as a feature of their programmes.

  Despite the locations of all the case study institutions being in areas with high minority ethnic populations, the unsystematic way in which practice experience is provided for students leads to a failure to maximize potential learning opportunities. That this should be so in institutions chosen for their positive response to addressing the issues of ethnic diversity only serves to emphasize our concern with the haphazard allocation of learning opportunities identified in the national survey. Teachers, students, practitioners and mentors appear to feel similarly disempowered in addressing the problem they identify. Each laments the haphazard way in which practice experience is organized, yet none of these groups claims a role or an authority in influencing or facilitating change. Nevertheless, the centrality of practice experience to students' learning is highly regarded. There is a common agreement that sources of expertise in the area of ethnicity are significantly located within lay communities, and these must be nurtured and maximized. This was a view echoed by three out of four focus groups in case study 1, seven of the 12 in case study 2 and five out of eight in case study 3. A complementary statement is found in the confident expression that where students are able to meet minority ethnic clients, and their significant others, then learning about diverse needs takes place. However, caution is required in assuming that what is being learned is an appropriate contribution to the development of transcultural competence.

Echoing the concern with racism that was identified in the synoptic analysis of the focus group interviews, in the content analysis there was a strong indication that the practice context was affected by racism. Students, teachers, mentors and practitioners all make worrying reference to having witnessed racism in education and professional practice. Indeed, 10 of the 12 focus groups in case study 2 and six of the eight focus groups in case study 3 reported having witnessed racism in clinical practice or the college. Only in the more compact department of midwifery in case study 1 is this response much less prevalent, with only one focus group out of four reporting the experience. It is of some concern that none of these groups was able to express confidence in their own abilities to respond to such incidences in a constructive emancipatory way. This is particularly significant given the witnessing of racism in educational and professional practice, ranked as the most commonly occurring anxiety about working with minority ethnic clients and staff. It suggests a level of conscious incompetence which must be stressful to negotiate in a professional context where, as the national survey suggests, addressing ethnic diversity is not a consensual priority within professional education. Additionally, it is an important reminder that the skills and conviction involved in challenging racism among colleagues or clients are not necessarily the same as those which may underpin transcultural practice with a client.

A further concern evident in the content analysis is the identification of language barriers as a recurrent problem in appropriate nursing and midwifery care. Half of the focus groups in case study 1, seven of the 12 in case study 2 and six of the eight in case study 3 raised language as a major issue in the delivery of professional care. This, together with the lack of confidence in addressing racism in the professional environment, is indicative of a need to develop anti-oppressive and transcultural competencies that are sustained in both educational and practice settings.

By separating out responses relating to practice areas according to the different programmes, it is possible to identify features of the particular professional specialities, which in themselves support the notion of nursing and midwifery being a heterogeneous rather than an homogeneous grouping. For example, among midwives, their relationship to their minority ethnic community clients appears to be one in which a system of shared learning and respect of difference may be developed and refined into a level of competence. This can be recognized in their common identification of such clients as both a source of expertise and a learning resource, and also in their confidence in feeling prepared to meet the needs of minority ethnic clients, or having the resources to improve their own sense of adequacy. For example, six out of the eight midwifery groups interviewed agreed that they felt adequately prepared to meet and/or teach the health care needs of minority ethnic communities, whereas only two of the eight adult branch focus groups and three out of eight mental health branch focus groups answered as positively.

Perhaps critics may suggest that midwives find themselves in the unique position of having some months to set up a relationship with their clients prior to the advent of the event wherein the practitioner must provide significant support. It is of course the case that a nurse caring for a sick adult, or a client who is mentally ill, tends first to meet that client and his or her significant others in circumstances normatively defined as illness, with all that is associated with that label. However, what is clear is the importance of getting to know the local community, the manner in which they live and their personal expectations. This is a knowledge base which the midwives appeared to value. In addition, the sense of cohesiveness and *esprit des corps*, highlighted earlier in this chapter, gives the midwife respondents a confidence in their own abilities to support one another and to learn from one another's individual networks in order to ensure personal development. This example of practitioners supporting practitioners is a prominent feature of the analysis of the midwifery data, but sadly is not as clearly expressed in an analysis of the nursing programmes.

In respect of each of the three programmes, there is a clear indication across the case study sites of the value placed by students on learning from minority ethnic clients and their relatives. Furthermore, the knowledge and expertise gained from working with minority ethnic staff is seen as a valuable learning resource. The implications that this has for minority ethnic persons are explored in the following chapter.

Curriculum issues

The different focus groups across the three case study sites generally considered the college-based component of the programmes as only being able to establish an awareness of issues of ethnic diversity, rather than an in-depth knowledge of the subject, with 16 out of the 24 focus groups making this point. This position may in part be explained by the strong indication across the three case studies that topics which might inform an understanding of the health care needs of minority ethnic communities appeared to be permeated throughout the taught component of the curriculum rather than being taught as discrete subjects. However, it was difficult to deduce exactly how permeation was conceptualized by participants, particularly as commonly identified learning opportunities relating to the classroom are distinctly discrete. For example, levels of agreement between participants would suggest that organized visits to minority ethnic community centres and visiting speakers are both noted for their value in facilitating learning, with all the focus groups in case study 1, three-quarters in case study 2, and four out of eight in case study 3 supporting this view.

In discussions of ideas for the further development of programmes, 'bringing in outside speakers' emerged as the most commonly agreed suggestion. Permeation as a popular response therefore opens up for discussion the manner in which its existence can be sustained in the college-based component of the curriculum. However, the responsibility each individual must take in the development of knowledge relating to the needs of minority ethnic clients appears to be significant for ensuring skills in this area are developed. What is arguable is whether experiences seen as valuable learning opportunities are essentially identified directly as a result of professional education or of living in an ethnically diverse society. For example, personal and social interaction is seen as a common and valued opportunity for students, teachers, mentors and practitioners, through which they can develop transcultural competence. Similarly, meeting minority ethnic clients and staff in practice placements has a strongly positive influence on learning, as does the use of learning materials, such as books or videos. It could be suggested, therefore, that the collection of personal and shared experiences communicated in the classroom provides a medium for ensuring the presence of ethnicity as an important theme running through programmes. To some extent this may provide an answer to the confusion which seems to emerge surrounding permeation as a concept, i.e. it suggests that permeation as a deliberate educational strategy is not seen to be taking place. Rather, what participants in each centre have in common is an understanding of the importance of bringing experiences to the educational setting, in effect inserting the topic into an already established professional education agenda. There is also the notion that clinical experience becomes part of classroom-based discussion; therefore practice and theory enjoy a tentative link which is highly dependent on individuals for its survival.

That the success or failure of addressing ethnicity in the curriculum depends largely upon the commitment of individuals was a feature of the survey results. Again this is reflected in the participants' collective approach to the development of their own personal skills. Common agreement was expressed that each person had the opportunity to further develop his or her skills in this area, yet there was little evidence of organization in the way such opportunities were presented. Continuing the theme of individual responsibility, participants generally looked towards their own resourcefulness; for example, 10 out of the 15 groups identifying potential for personal development cited engaging in private study or challenging their own professional practice as the means through which they could seize such opportunities.

In many respects this reflects a professional ethos which made a strong impression on the research team during the collection of data: namely, that participants repeatedly echoed the notion of treating the individual within the framework of holistic care. Thus the picture which emerges is one in which participants emphasize the importance of individual self reliance. To this end, the concept of individualism acts as a means of ensuring the development and maintenance of a suitable knowledge base, and also becomes a philosophy for delivering care which is deemed appropriate to specific clients.

Here differences between the programmes appear as structural approaches to the delivery of education in this area. The tendency towards a preference for permeating issues throughout curricula is complemented by an equal distribution of specific input in the midwifery courses. This finding is specific to midwifery and may reflect a more confident willingness to explore issues of ethnicity and the needs of minority ethnic clients routinely in educational provision. Furthermore, the relationship between minority ethnic users and educational providers is apparent in a commitment to engaging users in curriculum development, a process which was absent in the nursing programmes.

The mental health branch participants across case studies expressed a strong investment in the value of self-directed learning as a means of acquiring transcultural competence. Importance was placed on providing students with opportunities to pursue the health care needs of minority ethnic clients; for example, through written course work. However, these opportunities were not a requirement and students could exercise a degree of choice over whether to pursue them or not. A perhaps related finding more appropriate to the mental health programmes was a high degree of consensus that more minority ethnic staff needed to be recruited to mental health nursing, emphasizing the value of the life experience of such persons in providing care and in supporting students' learning.

Conclusion

When we reflect on the evidence presented in this chapter, from both the synoptic analysis and the content analysis, it is apparent that substantial similarities emerge across the nursing specialisms and midwifery, and across institutions, in the issues which emerge as common priorities. There is an indication that the ethnic demography of the city in which the institution is located plays a significant role in making ethnic diversity an issue within the curriculum. This has worrying implications in relation to our national survey, where too many institutions felt able virtually to ignore the issue on account of local demography. And evidence in this chapter that trusts were instrumental in requiring this to be addressed within education institutions is also likely to be responsive to the trusts' own demographic profiles as they address the needs of their client populations. Consequently, there is a need for professional and statutory bodies to take a lead in making this a national rather than a local issue. This is perhaps critically so, given the unambiguous evidence from current teachers and mentors that many do not feel competent in being able to teach transcultural competencies. The lack of transcultural competence and confidence within the current nursing professions indicates the need for a systematic provision of post-registration continuing education. This is a responsibility for trust management to take up: as is the responsibility to address the image of inadequate provision for minority ethnic clients which is presented by the nursing professionals in this study. As we argued in Chapter 2, individual practitioners' transcultural competence is not adequate compensation for inequitable policies and resource allocation within health care institutions.

Running through the data presented in this chapter is a clear indication of the critical role which practice settings play within the programmes. They are seen as the fulcrum around which the other elements of the programme must pivot; they are the crucible in which the elements of course-based learning are melted into practice competencies. As yet it is apparent that even in these selected case studies the happenstance entry into placements, which was such a theme of the national survey, is characteristic of professional education. The opportunity for students to work with minority ethnic clients and colleagues is universally valued, yet left largely to chance. Related issues arise in the identification of the enabling of students to have contact with minority ethnic communities and of having persons from these communities brought into the curriculum as visiting lecturers.

Clearly, minority ethnic persons, as colleagues, teachers, clients or social acquaintances, emerge as one and perhaps the most, valued resource in professional education and training. Yet if these persons are not to be exploited and abused, and if they are not to become a panacea for the majority professionals' failure to take responsibility for their acquisition of transcultural skills as teachers and practitioners, then great care must be taken. The evidence from these case studies suggests that there is not yet a sufficiently coherent management structure for this issue to be thought through and planned in a way which integrates the educational institution and the practice experience. At present there appears to be an *ad hoc* and pragmatic exploitation of these highly valued placements and community contacts, which fails to respect fully the integrity of these persons as individuals; nor has their full participation in shaping their communities' contribution to professional education been facilitated appropriately.

The frequency with which racism in the practice setting has emerged in the synoptic analysis and the content analysis underlines this point. If the institutional culture still enables racism to be a tolerable component of nursing and midwifery care then individual nurses' transcultural competencies are very seriously compromised. Chapter 3 indicated how devastating, and extensive in their impact, individual acts of racism may be. Individual transcultural skills must be complemented by institutional equal opportunity and anti-oppressive policies which exclude racism from health care environments. This would include the imposition of specific prescriptions against explicit racist behaviour, and policies which identify and remove unintended forms of institutional racism.

Issues around the recruitment and retention of minority ethnic staff, which are discussed in the next chapter, are one instance where institutional racism has been a focus of concern. But the data in this chapter may perhaps have suggested another potential area for concern. Language difficulties in working across cultural boundaries emerge as a major issue of the participants in the focus groups, and are equally important in the users' accounts of their experiences of care. While this study has not been able to examine extensively the quality of language support available through interpreter services and link workers, the suggestion is that it is far from adequate. A collusive willingness to tolerate this situation by health service purchasers and providers seriously compromises the efforts of committed nurses and midwives who seek to acquire transcultural competencies.

In concluding this chapter, it would be wrong to have implied that the data presented here offer only the basis for a litany of negative experiences. It is clear that substantial efforts are being made to prepare nurses and midwives to work effectively with a multi-ethnic clientele. The written word cannot reflect the personal commitment and energy that the researchers found among individuals in our case study institutions. And as our data above have indicated, there is an entirely laudable willingness on the part of students and existing teachers and practitioners to be honestly reflexive in their examination of their own and their profession's response to addressing the health care needs of an ethnically diverse society. However, a willingness to develop conscientiously an equitable health care system for all, irrespective of their ethnic identity, is not universally present within the nursing professions. But at the level of senior management and at grass roots level, there is a small cohort that have addressed this issue, and upon which further initiatives for improvement may be built.

6

Recruiting minority ethnic students into the nursing professions

Introduction

The inequalities which exist between ethnic groups regarding the extent to which health care services are responsive to their needs are well recognized and have been highlighted in earlier chapters. Equitable access for minority ethnic persons into careers in health care has also received considerable attention in recent times and is acknowledged to be a problem which needs to be addressed (King Edward's Hospital Fund for London 1990; DoH 1993b). To this end, it has been suggested that the inequalities in health care provision may be partially remedied by employing minority ethnic health care staff who share the cultural and linguistic characteristics of the populations they serve, and are therefore arguably better placed to identify and respond to health care needs (Rashid 1990). It is from these perspectives that it is appropriate, within a study which examines the educational preparation of nurses and midwives to practice in a multi-ethnic society, to give some consideration to the recruitment of students from different ethnic backgrounds into nursing and midwifery education.

This chapter provides an account of the particular stage of the study which examined the ethnic background of students entering nursing and midwifery education. We begin by providing an overview of the main issues to arise from a review of the literature concerning the recruitment of people from minority ethnic communities into the nursing and midwifery professions. In recognizing the dearth of empirical research in this area, together with the lack of valid data on the ethnic composition on the nursing professions, we readily acknowledge the difficulties of attempting to undertake this analysis. We then move on to consider the methods employed in this stage of the study. Specifically, we sought to analyse data collated by the ENB on the ethnic background of applicants to nursing and midwifery programmes and to explore the views of managers within the three case study institutions regarding factors influencing the recruitment of students from minority ethnic backgrounds.

The ethnic composition of the NHS: issues of recruitment and retention

Although the NHS is purported to be the largest employer of people from minority ethnic communities in Britain (Ward 1993), evidence relating to the actual numbers of qualified nurses and midwives drawn from different minority ethnic populations is at present fragmentary, as it is only comparatively recently that systematic ethnic monitoring has been introduced. Health service providers have previously not been required to monitor the ethnic background of their employees and the UKCC, which maintains records of all registered nurses and midwives, has only recently made a decision to start recording the ethnic background of newly qualified practitioners. However, it is likely to be some time before accurate figures for the total nursing workforce are available. Furthermore, although in 1990 the ENB began to collect data on the ethnic background of applicants to pre-registration nursing and midwifery programmes, changes in the ethnic monitoring procedures adopted by the ENB have meant that these data are at present incomplete.

Notwithstanding the lack of a national overview of the ethnic mix of the nursing workforce, there is some evidence to suggest that, on the whole, minority ethnic persons may be over-represented in nursing in comparison to the general population. A recent extensive survey of over 14,000 nurses, undertaken on behalf of the Department of Health (Beishon *et al.* 1995), identified that of the 62 per cent of nurses responding, approximately 8 per cent were drawn from minority ethnic backgrounds, as opposed to 6 per cent of the population at large (OPCS 1992). However, a more detailed breakdown of ethnic origin indicates that particular ethnic groups may be over-represented while others appear under-represented. Of those nurses identifying themselves as being of minority ethnic origin, 4 per cent were from Black minority groups, 2 per cent from Asian and 2 per cent from other ethnic backgrounds. In this context Black was defined as including Black, Black African and Black Caribbean, Asian as including Bangladeshi, Indian and Pakistani and the category 'other' as incorporating the remaining groups. These figures contrast with a national overview, whereby approximately 2 per cent of the population are from Black minority backgrounds, 3.5 per cent Asian and 1 per cent of other ethnic origin (OPCS 1992). However, as we will highlight later in this chapter, there are a number of limitations with presenting data on ethnic identity in this way, and a degree of caution needs to be exercised in interpreting the significance of such data.

Despite the relatively high proportion of minority ethnic nurses, there have been a number of claims that they are disproportionately concentrated among lower grade nursing posts (Akinsanya 1988; Ward 1993). However, Beishon *et al.*'s (1995) findings question these assertions by identifying that minority ethnic nurses did not appear to be disadvantaged in accessing middle-ranking clinical posts (up to grade E). Indeed, Asian nurses appear more likely than their white counterparts to have reached grade E. However, Black nurses were seen to be at a significant disadvantage in gaining access to grades F and above, and there were also indications that Asian nurses were slightly slower in reaching these senior positions. Beishon *et al.* (1995) also indicate that minority ethnic personnel were not evenly distributed over the nursing professions, being particularly visible in mental health, elderly care and medical and surgical areas, and less so in midwifery and children's nursing.

Alongside an acknowledgement of the shortfall in minority ethnic staff occupying senior nursing positions within the NHS has come a call to improve recruitment from minority ethnic communities; with attendant claims relating to the benefits this may bring to enhancing the services offered to minority ethnic clients (King Edward's Hospital Fund for London 1990). To this end, the government has recently launched an initiative detailing an action plan aimed at achieving 'equitable representation' of people from minority ethnic communities among senior clinical nursing grades. Specific goals for health care providers to achieve have been identified in relation to the overall recruitment of nurses from minority ethnic communities as well as their distribution within nursing specialities and grades (DoH 1993b). The rationale for this initiative is presented in terms of the need for the workforce to reflect the ethnic diversity of local populations in an effort to ensure that the health care needs of different sections of the community are appropriately met.

Clearly, if followed through, this initiative has implications not just for health care providers but also for those involved in nurse education. However, while it is laudable, it fails to take account of the fact that a minority ethnic workforce may be Eurocentric in its practice on account of its pre-registration education programmes. If minority ethnic practitioners are socialized into the white middle class norms which underpin British nursing practice (Stokes 1991), it is questionable as to whether they will be able to meet effectively the needs of minority ethnic clients. Furthermore, although the report specifies targets which are to be achieved, it fails to provide an analysis as to the reasons why people from minority ethnic communities are so poorly represented in senior positions or to present any guidance on the strategies which might be employed in an attempt to overcome this disadvantaged position. Arguably, the recruitment of minority ethnic staff into nursing is unlikely to improve without an understanding of the factors which influence recruitment and a commitment to taking active measures to remedy the situation.

The literature concerning the recruitment of minority ethnic staff into health professional careers in general, and nursing and midwifery in particular, is somewhat sparse. Although a number of authors express concern that recruitment may be poor from particular minority ethnic communities, few of their claims are based on large-scale empirical research. Rather, they appear to draw upon small-scale studies or anecdotal evidence. However, two discernible strands are evident in the literature as possible explanations as to why recruitment from minority ethnic communities may be low. The first relates to perceived cultural norms which may restrict people from certain ethnic communities, particularly Asian women, from pursuing a career in nursing or midwifery. The second refers to the impact of institutional racism within the NHS on the experiences and opportunities of people from minority ethnic communities who pursue health professional careers.

The literature relating to the effects that cultural norms may have on influencing career choices is somewhat limited and contradictory. Karseras and Hopkins (1987) suggest that the relatively poor image of nursing as a career option in comparison to other professions, such as medicine or law, dissuades potential applicants. This, they claim, is particularly so in Asian communities, where, it is argued, physical caring is held in low regard. However, although it may be the case that nurse recruitment is a problem in some Asian countries, the professional recognition and career structure of the nursing professions in Britain is quite different from that in Asian countries and does not appear to explain adequately why recruitment may be low. Karseras and Hopkins further suggest that recruitment is affected by religious and cultural barriers which militate against female nurses providing care to male clients. However, Ward (1993) challenges this assumption, arguing that Karseras and Hopkins make fairly major generalizations about a group of people who differ widely in culture, religion, beliefs and lifestyle. From a slightly different perspective, Bharj (1995), in an admittedly small-scale study, indicates that although the Asian school leavers she interviewed were not favourably disposed towards nursing as a career option, they were influenced not so much by cultural perceptions but by the way in which nursing has been portrayed in popular television dramas such as *Casualty* or documentaries on hospital life such as *Jimmy's*. Furthermore, Bharj challenges the assumption that cultural restrictions may prevent Asian nurses caring for male clients, as one of her respondents explained:

> My religion does restrict my coming into contact with males other than immediate family. However, this is related mainly to social gatherings. With regard to helping sick people, it is the duty of every individual to help others – if you enter a caring profession then it doesn't matter who you are caring for.
>
> (Bharj 1995: 42)

In addition to assumptions about the cultural appropriateness of the nursing professions as valued career options for people from minority ethnic communities, the literature raises questions as to the extent to which young people's career choices may be influenced by parents and the community.

However, strong claims, such as those recently made by Cassidy (1995), that Asian parents consider young women who take up nursing as a career to be severely disadvantaged in respect of opportunities for marriage, are unsubstantiated by empirical data. Indeed, the part that parents may play in influencing their children's career choice is far from clear, although it appears that the process of social change within Asian communities is complexly affecting the extent to which parental influence impacts upon a number of life choices which young people make (see, for example, Afshar 1994). Thus it is of concern that much of the literature relating to the effects of cultural influences on the recruitment of students from minority ethnic communities into nursing appears to be anecdotal and, alarmingly, it portrays cultural stereotypes, particularly of Asian communities, which are unsubstantiated and remain largely unchallenged. Although it may be that cultural beliefs and practices exert some influence, there appears to be an overarching failure to recognize that the religious, cultural and socio-economic heterogeneity within Asian communities may mean that there is a variety of perspectives on the cultural appropriateness of nursing as a career choice, rather than a predominance of a single perspective.

In contrast to the perspectives which stress cultural norms as the main obstacle to recruitment from minority ethnic communities into nursing and midwifery, a number of authors suggest that the problem resides in the institutional racism that permeates both the health service and educa-tion institutions providing nursing and midwifery education (Akinsanya 1988; Baxter 1988; Lee Cumin 1989; Bharj 1995). Ward (1993) argues that people's views of the NHS are not merely a product of cultural beliefs but also relate to their experiences of and within the health service. In this respect, the nursing professions have a somewhat chequered history and are not portrayed in a very favourable light.

In response to an acute shortage of nurses in the 1960s and early 1970s, active measures were taken by the government to recruit from the British ex-colonies. The move was successful insofar as a large number of people, particularly young women, entered the health service. However, upon ar-rival in Britain, many applicants found themselves working as untrained nursing auxiliaries in the less popular areas of health care, such as elderly care, mental health or learning disabilities. Those who managed to secure a place in nurse training were frequently channelled into State Enrolled Nurse (SEN) courses rather than the more prestigious State Registered Nurse (SRN) courses. This was despite a significant proportion having the appropriate academic qualifications to pursue SRN training (Ward 1993). Once qualified, the nurses frequently encountered difficulty secur-ing posts other than in the less attractive specialisms, and opportunities for promotion were severely restricted (Butler 1993). The legacy that these experiences created is still seen to exert an influence on potential recruits today. Indeed, parental influence may not be so much a matter of impos-ing adherence to cultural expectations but may be a reaction to earlier experiences of racism (Torkington 1987).

McNaught (1994) claims that the position of minority ethnic staff has changed little in the intervening years. Although there have been some initiatives aimed at addressing the problem, improvements have been marginal, with cases of discriminatory employment practices being regularly reported (McKeigure *et al.* 1991; Esmail and Everington 1993; Nursing Times 1995). These views are supported by the findings of a number of recent reports on employment of minority ethnic staff in the NHS (Akinsanya 1988; King Edward's Hospital Fund for London 1990). However, Beishon *et al.*'s (1995) recent study suggests that the positions occupied by minority ethnic staff may be shifting slightly, in that although they confirm the continued non-random distribution of minority ethnic nurses across specialisms, they appear to indicate relatively good career prospects for nurses up to and including the mid-range posts. Notwithstanding this seemingly positive change, it is of concern that Beishon *et al.* also identify an increase in the reporting of racial discrimination among minority ethnic staff, in contrast to their white counterparts, and a significant proportion of minority ethnic nurses experiencing racial harassment from both colleagues and clients. The consequent need for employers to address the inequalities and discrimination faced by minority ethnic staff pursuing a career within the NHS is highlighted in a number of Race Relations Codes of Practice produced by the Commission for Racial Equality (CRE 1984, 1989, 1992, 1994). However, these documents have no legal standing and are merely guidelines for best practice which may or may not be taken up by health service employers or education institutions. Although many NHS employers do have equal opportunity policies, there is often a significant gap between policy and the actual practices undertaken in the workplace (Beishon *et al.* 1995). In a broader sense, the capacity of equal opportunity policies to modify the location of minority ethnic personnel within the British labour force has been depressingly modest (Jenkins and Solomos 1989). This suggests that recruitment, training and promotion opportunities for minority ethnic practitioners may be unfair.

The recruitment practices of colleges of nursing and midwifery have also been criticized for their failure to address adequately equal opportunity issues in facilitating the recruitment of students from minority ethnic backgrounds (King Edward's Hospital Fund for London 1990). In a study examining racial equality in nursing and midwifery education, Butler (1993) noted that 13 per cent of colleges surveyed did not have an equal opportunity policy in force despite it being a requirement of the ENB for the approval of institutions (ENB 1993). Of those that did have a declared policy, there were major limitations in respect of how the policy was implemented and subsequently monitored. Butler goes on to suggest that unless appropriate and effective equal opportunity policies are in place potential applicants from minority ethnic backgrounds may continue to be deterred from entering the nursing and midwifery professions.

In addition to considering the need to increase the recruitment of students from minority ethnic communities into nursing, it is important to consider the retention of such students on nursing and midwifery programmes. Day (1994) claims that not only do well qualified candidates from minority ethnic communities find it more difficult to secure training places on professional courses, they are also more likely to drop out of the course or fail the examinations. Again, the literature in this area is patchy, with most of it emanating from North America, and, by and large, it does not appear to be based on empirical research. Rather, authors have provided evaluative accounts of some of the specific initiatives they have taken forward in an attempt to improve retention rates. Notwithstanding these limitations, this literature does serve to provide some tentative pointers to some of the issues that merit consideration by nurse educators in the UK.

Commenting on the higher attrition rates among Black students on nursing programmes in the USA, Jones (1992) suggests that psychological, economic, social and organizational factors may all play a part. Marshall (1989) further identifies the importance of social networks, the size and composition of student cohorts and the relationship between students and lecturing staff as affecting retention rates. In an attempt to counter these influences, pre-college and induction programmes are seen to provide students with a realistic insight into what nurse education entails (Jones 1992). In addition, the potential benefits of mentorship programmes designed specifically to support students from minority ethnic communities are highlighted (Weekes 1989; Baldwin and Wold 1993; Williams and Rogers 1993), with Alvarez and Abriam-Yago (1993) reporting on the particular success of a scheme which matched students from minority ethnic communities with a mentor who was a qualified nurse drawn from the same minority ethnic community.

Recognition of the effects that lecturing staff may exert on minority ethnic students' experiences of nurse education is also considered in the North American literature. Jones (1992) refers to a number of studies in the USA which indicate that lecturing staff treat Black students differently from white students on account of the perceptions they have of these students, which are shaped by racial stereotypes. In particular, lecturing staff are seen to portray lower expectations of participation by students from minority groups in class discussions. However, the corollary of this is that Black students are frequently expected by staff not only to act as experts on matters relating to ethnicity but also to represent their 'race' in discussions on ethnic diversity. This ethnocentric bias is further apparent in predominantly 'white' schools, where although it is common to find academic expressions of intolerance for overtly racist behaviours, position statements detailing a commitment to ethnic and cultural diversity as a positive contributing source are less in evidence (Kavanagh et al. 1993). In such circumstances particular effort is required to facilitate positive interaction and to eliminate racism from the actions of the majority students and staff (Richardson 1989). To this end, it is suggested that carefully tailored staff development programmes, which provide the opportunity for staff to explore their own attitudes and behaviours towards minority ethnic students and consider the impact that this may have on the students they teach, may be instrumental in enabling lecturing staff to develop belief in the abilities of students from minority ethnic backgrounds and high expectations of academic achievement (Jones 1992). However, in this context the critique of shallow and tokenistic race awareness training programmes that proliferated in Britain in the late 1970s and early 1980s should be very carefully noted, and its implications for nursing and midwifery education heeded (Gurnah 1989; Sivanandan 1981).

The preceding review of the literature has served to highlight the lack of any comprehensive data concerning the ethnic composition of the nursing professions. Although there is an indication that the proportion of nurses from minority ethnic backgrounds is higher than that of the general population, they may be disproportionately concentrated in the lower and middle clinical grades and in the less attractive clinical specialities. It is also acknowledged that recruitment of minority ethnic students could be improved. The review has identified a notable lack of empirical studies examining factors influencing the recruitment and retention of minority ethnic students into nursing and midwifery education. In view of these deficits, it was anticipated that this stage of the study would begin to shed some light on a number of these issues.

Research methods

Recognizing the complexities surrounding the recruitment of students from minority ethnic communities into nursing and midwifery education, this stage of the research aimed to examine the range of ethnic backgrounds of students entering pre-registration nursing and midwifery programmes. In addition, it sought to identify the key factors perceived by education and service managers as influencing the recruitment of students from minority ethnic backgrounds. In accordance with the general focus of the study, data were sought specifically in relation to pre-registration diploma level courses in adult and mental health nursing and in midwifery.

With regard to examining the ethnic background of students entering nursing and midwifery programmes, statistical data providing a national overview of recruitment patterns were sought from the ENB. The application process to pre-registration diploma level programmes in nursing and midwifery education is managed by the National Central Clearing House (NCCH), which is administered by the ENB. All potential applicants are required to complete a standard application form, which is then forwarded to the institutions of their choice. Following the selection procedures carried out by the individual institutions, applicants may be offered a place on a course and the NCCH is notified accordingly. Applicants are then required to confirm their acceptance or otherwise of the offer. Upon taking up a place on a programme students are required to index with the ENB. It was anticipated at the outset of the study that it would be possible readily to access statistical data from the NCCH regarding the ethnic background of applicants, those who were subsequently offered a place and those who ultimately took up the offer. However, modifications in the recording of ethnic data on the application forms, together with the introduction of a new computerized system for storing ethnic data by the ENB, meant that at the time of undertaking the study only limited information was available.

In addition to an overview of the different patterns of recruitment of minority ethnic students as evidenced by the statistical data, we were keen to gain an understanding of some of the issues which education institutions faced in seeking to recruit minority ethnic students. We sought to ascertain the views of both education and service managers in the three case study sites regarding factors influencing recruitment and to identify any specific initiatives which were being taken forward in this area. In each of the institutions we interviewed the key education managers with lead responsibility for recruitment and selection. In addition, we explored these issues within the broader agenda of the semi-structured interviews we undertook with a range of education and service managers. A total of 32 interviews were undertaken, 18 with education managers and 14 with service managers. The interviews were tape recorded and subsequently transcribed. The transcripts were then separately coded by two independent researchers in order to identify issues which were common across case study sites and those which were specific to a particular institution.

Statistical data on the recruitment of students from minority ethnic groups

Only limited information relating to the ethnic backgrounds of applicants and those currently undertaking nursing and midwifery programmes was available from the ENB. Specifically, data relating to the ethnic background of students currently undertaking pre-registration diploma level programmes in adult and mental health nursing and midwifery were provided, together with the most recent data on the ethnic background of students entering the two nursing programmes. Notwithstanding these limitations, the data that were available present an interesting snapshot of the ethnic composition of student nurses and midwives currently in training and form a tentative basis for monitoring future trends. However, before we present these data it is important to consider briefly some methodological issues associated with the recording and subsequent interpretation of ethnic data.

Statistics on ethnic groupings are becoming a pervasive feature of contemporary health care research and policy making. In particular, they are seen to provide a means whereby access to, and utilization of, particular services can be monitored. The collection of ethnic data is often justified in terms of the role they can play in highlighting discriminatory practices, identifying action that should be taken and establishing how far existing policies having this objective have succeeded in improving the experiences of minority ethnic populations (Smaje 1995). It was with this intention in mind that the King Edward's Hospital Fund for London report (1990) argued for ethnic monitoring to be introduced as a means of overcoming the discrimination experienced by minority ethnic nurses, both in respect of their initial application to undertake nurse training and throughout the remainder of their career trajectory.

The model of ethnic classification employed by the ENB is that advocated by the Department of Health. The coding is based on a national minimum standard for classifying ethnic groups, using the categories derived from the 1991 Census. Nine categories are identified, eight of which relate to specific identified groups, with the ninth being a residual category encompassing all 'other ethnic groups'. People completing the form are asked to classify themselves on the basis of the ethnic group that best describes their self-perceived identity.

However, although the collection of ethnic data is advocated by some, there is a developing critique which challenges their use on political, theoretical and practical grounds. In a comprehensive analysis of the use of ethnicity as a measurement in health research, Sheldon and Parker (1992) identify a number of concerns with its current usage. In particular, the 1991 Census categories raise problems with consistency of measurement, as they are derived on the basis of different criteria; for example, on the basis of colour (black, white), notions of nationality (e.g. Pakistani, Indian) and geographical location (African, Caribbean). A further limitation is that the categories take no account of the changing nature of ethnic identity. The fluidity of the boundaries demarcating ethnic groups poses the problem of how such a dynamic entity can be measured. To this end, the prescriptive nature of ethnic categories appears inflexible to changes in ethnic identity over time and ignores the fact that people may not always classify themselves in the same way (Smaje 1995). Sheldon and Parker conclude that insofar as ethnicity can be measured, it can only reflect a transient snapshot and is therefore of limited use in planning.

Additionally, there is no provision within the classification system for those who categorize themselves as 'other ethnic group' to write a description of their ethnic identity. Aspinall (1995) contends that providing people with the opportunity to define their ethnic group in their own terms acknowledges the complex way in which people perceive, identify and articulate ethnic membership. He also claims that the current approach is flawed in respect of the ideological and practical drawbacks which force people into standard ethnic categories. This is particularly so for an increasing number of people of 'mixed parentage' (with parents from different ethnic groups), who do not feel catered for by the predefined categories. They are required to choose which ethnic group they identify with most rather than provide a description of what they consider their ethnic origin to be. The subsequent reification of ethnic origin, without an acknowledgment

Table 6.1 Ethnic origin of students undertaking pre-registration diploma programmes in adult nursing, mental health nursing and midwifery as of November 1995

Ethnic group	Number of students	Percentage of students in training	Aggregate percentage of students in training
White	19,658	91.80	91.80
Black Caribbean	203	0.95 ⎫	
Black African	499	2.33 ⎬	3.62
Black	72	0.34 ⎭	
Indian	182	0.85 ⎫	
Pakistani	50	0.23 ⎬	1.18
Bangladeshi	21	0.10 ⎭	
Chinese	42	0.20 ⎫	1.43
Other	263	1.23 ⎭	
Non-specified	422	1.97	1.97
Total in training	21,412	100	100

Source: ENB.

of the dynamic and changing nature of ethnic identity, may give rise to social groups which are artefactual and have no real meaning. The reader needs to take account of such methodological issues associated with ethnic monitoring and exercise a degree of caution in interpreting the ethnic data on student recruitment presented below.

In respect of the three programmes which provided the focus for this study, there were 21,412 students in training in November 1995; of these, the ethnic origin of 98 per cent was known. A total of 1,332 students (6 per cent) had classified themselves of minority ethnic origin, a figure which mirrors the percentage of minority ethnic people within the general population (OPCS 1992). Table 6.1 provides a breakdown of the ethnic origin of all the students in training. Because the proportions of students from some minority groups are particularly small, the percentages have also been shown as an aggregate of broader ethnic categories, although the limitations with this approach need to be acknowledged. The aggregate categories are those commonly used in other reports on ethnic monitoring (Beishon *et al.* 1995) and are as follows: 'Black', encompassing Black Caribbean, Black African and Black; 'Asian', encompassing Indian, Pakistani and Bangladeshi; and an extension of the category 'other' to include Chinese.

The aggregate figures indicate that approximately half of the students from minority ethnic backgrounds in training were Black, with the remainder approximately equally divided between Asian and other. Interestingly, these figures mirror the ethnic composition of nursing staff identified in

Table 6.2 The percentage of students from different ethnic groups undertaking pre-registration programmes of adult nursing, mental health nursing and midwifery as of November 1995

Ethnic group	Adult nursing	Mental health nursing	Midwifery
White	93.1	84.7	92.8
Black	2.8	8.3	2.5
Asian	1.2	1.5	1.0
Other	1.2	2.7	0.7
Non-specified	1.7	2.8	3.0

Source: ENB.

Beishon *et al.*'s (1995) recent survey, which included both qualified and unqualified nursing staff but excluded students in training.

Table 6.2 provides a more detailed breakdown of the ethnic origin of students in training for each of the three programmes. The data indicate that the proportion of minority ethnic students undertaking mental health nurse training is greater than in adult nursing or midwifery. Approximately 12 per cent of mental health nursing students, in comparison to only 5 per cent of adult nursing students and 4 per cent of midwifery students, are from minority ethnic backgrounds. This difference can to a large extent be accounted for by the increased proportion of Black students in this branch of nursing. However, it is not clear from the data whether this is a result of deliberate choice on the part of the applicant or whether Black students find it easier to secure a place in mental health nurse training because it is less popular than adult nursing.

In 1993, the NCCH streamlined its application procedures by introducing a fixed application period during which all applications for the following 12 months needed to be received. This first fixed application period ran from October 1993 to September 1994, with applications being received by the NCCH during the period October 1993 to December 1993. By the beginning of the second fixed application period in October 1994, all these applications had been processed by institutions and students who had been offered places had begun to take them up. Only data relating to the ethnic origin of applicants to adult and mental health nursing programmes were available at the time of undertaking this study.

Table 6.3 provides a breakdown of the ethnic origin of applicants for the first fixed application period, together with details of those who had subsequently commenced training as of the end of October 1995. It should be noted that there may have been a small number of students who had been offered places on courses commencing after October 1995, and therefore their details do not appear.

The data indicate that of the 86 per cent of applicants who provided details of their ethnic origin, 11 per cent were from minority ethnic groups. However, the relative proportion of minority ethnic students who had ultimately

Table 6.3   Ethnic origin of applicants to pre-registration programmes of adult and mental health nursing for the fixed application period (October 1993 to September 1994)

Ethnic group	Total number of applicants	Percentage of applicants	Total number of applicants in training as of 31 October 1995	Percentage of applicants in training as of 31 October 1995
White	15,156	74.7	9,516	93.6
Black	1,486	7.3	381	3.8
Asian	314	1.6	93	0.9
Other	479	2.3	136	1.3
Non-specified	2,861	14.1	45	0.4
Total	20,296	100	10,171	100

Source: ENB.

commenced training by October 1995 comprised only 6 per cent of the total student population. This suggests that minority ethnic applicants are less likely to secure a place in nurse training than white applicants. However, these figures cannot be taken entirely at face value, as some account needs to be taken of the 14 per cent of applicants who chose not to declare their ethnic origin on application. The number of applicants from this category who secured a place and subsequently did declare their ethnic origin upon indexing is not known. It is therefore impossible to gauge what effect this may exert on overall patterns of recruitment.

An additional factor which impacts upon the interpretation of Table 6.3 concerns the proportion of overseas applicants. The data obtained from the ENB do not provide details of the number of overseas applicants. Although nursing and midwifery programmes in the UK are technically open to overseas students, recent changes in legislation mean that applicants may not be eligible for a work permit upon qualifying. A news report in the Nursing Times (1995) claimed that overseas applicants may not be offered places on nursing and midwifery programmes because it is thought unlikely that they will obtain a work permit upon completion. This position was confirmed by all the case study colleges, which indicated that in the past they had recruited a number of overseas students, particularly from African countries, but now no longer did so because of the difficulty students experienced in securing a work permit upon qualification. Furthermore, as the colleges were contracted by regional health authorities to train a specific number of nurses and midwives on the basis of local workforce planning estimates, education managers indicated that they felt obliged to offer places to applicants whom they felt confident would be eligible to secure employment upon completion of the programmes.

Table 6.4 The number of students undertaking adult and mental health nursing programmes expressed as a percentage of the number of applicants applying from each ethnic group

Ethnic group	Total number of applicants	Total number of applicants in training as of 31 October 1995	Percentage of applicants in training as of 31 October 1995
White	15,156	9,516	62.8
Black Caribbean	298	116	38.9
Black African	1,096	228	20.8
Black	92	37	40.2
Indian	237	60	25.3
Pakistani	63	26	41.3
Bangladeshi	14	7	50.0
Chinese	40	19	47.5
Other	439	117	26.7
Non-specified	2,861	45	1.6

Source: ENB.

The fact that all three case study colleges raised this issue suggests that it might apply nationally. If this is so, it may in part account for the smaller proportion of minority ethnic applicants securing places in comparison to white applicants. While at face value it may be an understandable response on the part of colleges to the political pressures they are experiencing, it has significant implications for Britain's role in the international market of professional education.

However, even taking these two factors into account, the percentage of students commencing training in each minority group relative to the percentage who applied strongly suggests that white applicants are more likely to secure a place on nursing programmes than minority ethnic applicants. Table 6.4 shows a breakdown of the number of students from each ethnic group expressed as a percentage of those applying from that group and suggests that Black African and Indian applicants are about three times less likely to secure a place on a programme than white students.

Factors influencing recruitment: the colleges' perspectives

In view of the paucity of research examining the recruitment of students from minority ethnic backgrounds into nursing and midwifery education, we were keen to explore the issues which education and service managers considered to be influential. There was a general consensus among education managers in all three colleges that there was insufficient representation of students from minority ethnic backgrounds in each of the programmes we examined. This view was aptly summed up by one of the mental health education managers:

> It has horrified me that we would recruit 190 students at a time and within the group there may be four or five individuals who were not white. I would then step out of the back door of the [college] where the students were coming into and the cultural mix was the exact opposite. I find it quite disturbing that we actually exist in a very culturally diverse community and yet our intakes represent very much the white middle class. (3.7.17)

There was widespread agreement that more active measures should be taken to increase the proportion of minority ethnic students so that they more accurately reflected the ethnic mix of the local population. This position was also supported by the majority of service managers, who spoke very positively of the benefits of employing qualified nurses or midwives from minority ethnic backgrounds whose cultural and linguistic characteristics matched those of the local population and whom they considered well able to respond to the needs of minority ethnic clients. In some instances, the impetus for increasing the recruitment of minority ethnic practitioners clearly came from the service managers. However, as we argued in previous chapters, although the recruitment of minority ethnic staff may form part of an overall strategy designed to meet the health care needs of minority ethnic communities, it has major limitations.

Although there was general acknowledgement of a need to increase recruitment from minority ethnic communities, education managers appeared unsure as to how this might most effectively be achieved. A major difficulty which all three colleges faced in respect of their programmes was that the number of applicants who possessed the minimum entry requirements far exceeded the number of places on offer. The UKCC determines the minimum formal qualifications recognized for entry into both nursing and midwifery programmes. This is currently set at five GCSE passes at grade C or above, or their equivalent. It also provides for a number of alternative routes for those who do not possess the minimum educational requirements: these include access to higher education courses, national vocational qualifications and an educational test (the DC test) intended for mature students who do not possess formal qualifications. Beyond these minimum requirements, education institutions may set their own additional entry criteria.

The large number of suitably qualified applicants was seen to cause something of a dilemma. With the general upgrading of nursing and midwifery programmes to .diploma level, several education managers felt under pressure to recruit the most academically qualified students, on the assumption that they would be best able to cope with the theoretical component of the programme. However, despite this concern there was widespread acknowledgement that someone who was not highly qualified academically may possess the necessary personal attributes to make a 'good' nurse or midwife but, owing to the perceived pressure to recruit academically strong students, may be denied the opportunity to undertake training. Consequently, where minority ethnic students who may have much to offer the nursing professions have suffered from negative experiences at school, they may be disproportionately lost to the profession. All three colleges indicated that in the past they had been prepared to recruit students who were considered to be 'academic risks' and who might experience difficulty in completing the theoretical component of the programme, but who had demonstrated a number of other attributes which, on balance, were felt to compensate for academic deficiencies. With the upgrading of programmes to diploma level a number of education managers were unsure as to the wisdom of continuing with this course of action. There also appeared to be a general assumption that minority ethnic applicants were more likely to be academically less qualified than white applicants and, by effectively raising the entry requirements above the minimum specified, it may serve to disadvantage them further. This was particularly so of inner-city areas, where in one of the case studies education managers were aware of the county council's data on low achievement among minority ethnic students from inner-city schools. Interestingly, in this college there was a stronger commitment against raising the entry criteria above the minimum specified by the UKCC. However, the perceived under-achievement among minority ethnic school children is not fully borne out by the educational literature, which highlights the current high academic achievement of some minority ethnic school leavers nationally. This is particularly so among Indian and Chinese students, who have been seen to be out-performing white students (Modood and Shiner 1994).

In view of the expressed commitment to increase recruitment from minority ethnic communities, yet recognizing that programmes were heavily subscribed to, we were keen to explore the respondents' views on taking positive action to increase the proportion of minority ethnic students. Although the Race Relations Act 1976 does not allow for those involved in education or employment to discriminate when recruiting, it does permit positive action whereby members of a particular ethnic group can be provided with access to opportunities for training for specific work, or encouraged to take advantage of opportunities for doing that work when they have been under-represented in that area. The Department of Health (DoH 1993b) advocates the use of positive action in recruiting nurses and midwives from specific ethnic groups, where there is a clear service delivery need. However, the majority of both education and service managers seemed unsure as to whether positive action was an appropriate step to take. In many instances there appeared to be some misunderstanding in interpreting what was meant by positive action within the context of the Race Relations Act, confusing it with discriminating against other potential applicants, as one education manager explained:

I've got mixed views on positive action. Maybe it's because I'm not sure I understand the legality of issues about positive discrimination. If people are out there and they are eligible and they want to come, then we should be doing everything we can to help them in. But whether we earmark places for candidates from ethnic minorities – I guess I've not got any strong views although I think I'm leaning towards considering it inappropriate to do so, because I believe that people should get in on their merits. (3.9.6)

This position was further supported by a strong commitment towards treating all applicants as equals, irrespective of their ethnicity: 'I think everybody should be treated as an equal and provided everybody's got the same qualifications and meet the criteria, then everybody should have the same chance. If you possess the qualities they are looking for, whether it is a place on a course or a job, then you should be offered it' (1.4.16).

However, the same service manager went on to suggest that this did not always happen in practice, and on the basis of anecdotal evidence suspected that minority ethnic applicants may be disadvantaged. The suspicion appears to be borne out by the data from the ENB, which indicate that minority ethnic applicants are less likely than white applicants to secure a place in nursing and midwifery education and suggest that recruitment practices may be discriminatory. The fact that the colleges did not appear either to be aware of or to understand the opportunities available within the Race Relations Act actively to recruit minority ethnic students to train for particular areas where they are under-represented serves further to disadvantage minority ethnic applicants.

A number of reasons were put forward to account for the relatively low recruitment from minority ethnic communities into the nursing professions. Both education and service managers identified the poor image of nursing and midwifery as a career choice as being the major reason why potential recruits may be deterred. The views expressed by respondents as to why this should be the case were consistent with those expressed in the literature: namely, that becoming a nurse or midwife was not valued as a suitable career choice, particularly among Asian communities, because of its perceived low status, as one service manager outlined. 'It's not a high profile job. If you are going into health care you become a doctor not a nurse. There's no status in a lot of countries for nursing as a profession and, indeed, midwifery' (1.1.14). Alternatively, parental influence was seen to be an important factor, on account of cultural beliefs or practices:

Asian parents do not seem to see nursing as an appropriate profession for their daughters. It seems to be the family that are putting people off. I think it's the cultural view of the work of a nurse which puts people off. It depends on how strong someone's religious views are as to whether they'll let their daughter become a nurse. (2.11.3)

There are cultural differences – differences in whether women go out to work in the first place and what type of education they're going to have for that. There are many instances of arranged marriages and being shipped off home. I think there are probably quite a few people who aren't given the opportunity to look for a career because of their culture. (1.2.16)

Although there was some acknowledgement that second and third generation minority ethnic citizens may hold different views to the cultural stereotypes expressed above, the fact that these perceptions were so much in evidence suggests that managers reflect the ignorance identified in much of the literature; that is, that diversity exists not only between ethnic groups but importantly also within a particular group, and failure to acknowledge such diversity serves only to perpetuate ill-founded stereotypes. Unless there is an appreciation of the need to gain an accurate understanding of minority ethnic communities' perceptions of nursing as a career, then it is unlikely the recruitment initiatives will meet the success.

The negative experiences that minority ethnic persons may have had of the health service, either as service users or as employees, were also seen to dissuade potential applicants. Both education and service managers acknowledged the effects of individual and institutional racism within the health service. The legacy of disadvantage and discrimination arising from the overseas recruitment drives of the 1970s and the current experiences of racism encountered by minority ethnic staff and clients were seen as powerful influences dissuading potential applicants from minority ethnic backgrounds, as one manager explained:

One particular influence which is particularly strong is the historical one. In the 1970s we had deliberate recruitment policies from abroad because we couldn't staff our hospitals. What happened to those staff? Few went beyond enrolled nurses. We are now faced with their children and grandchildren. There is an important message for us here. 'There is no way I want my children to experience what I experienced in the NHS,' not taking on board that things have changed and we do things at least a little better now. (3.1.6)

This manager went on to highlight what for her was an important issue in ultimately encouraging recruitment from minority ethnic groups, namely the need to build links with minority ethnic communities in order to understand why more people from these communities do not pursue health professional careers: 'People talk about recruitment and retention; for me it starts way before recruitment and that is where the root of the problem is. It is about what the ethnic minority community actually know about the health service, what their view of the health service is, and believe me it is not good' (3.1.6). However, this was the only college which had sought to establish links with local minority ethnic communities and these were still in the early stages of development.

Each of the three colleges was attempting to address the shortfall in minority ethnic recruitment, with different degrees of activity. All of them were involved with attending careers conventions organized by local schools and with organizing their own open days for prospective applicants. However, the majority of these activities were not directed specifically at encouraging recruitment from minority ethnic communities. The colleges also highlighted the importance of having effective equal opportunity policies in place and of training staff involved in recruitment and selection in the effective execution of these policies. To this end, they had all established working groups responsible for reviewing the effectiveness of their policies, and the institution in case study 3 had gone as far as to review its selection criteria with the assistance of an inner city initiative group concerned with promoting opportunities for minority ethnic persons. However, the effectiveness of some of these initiatives was questioned by participants in each of the colleges and the need for evaluation was noted.

The college in case study 1 was the least active in respect of taking active measures to promote recruitment from minority ethnic communities. This is interesting bearing in mind that this college's curriculum was perceived by both students and staff to be the most coherent in facilitating an understanding of the needs of minority ethnic clients. While the college managers could identify a number of potential activities which might facilitate minority ethnic recruitment (for example, an access course offered by the local college of further education and college open days), none was targeted specifically at encouraging interest from potential minority ethnic applicants.

By contrast, the managers in case study 2 identified a number of initiatives which were targeted specifically at promoting minority ethnic recruitment. These included the following.

- Participating in the county council's ethnic minority annual job fair.
- Providing in-house open days designed to attract potential applicants from minority ethnic communities.
- Translating specific information on the college and its programmes into four local community languages. This literature was designed to provide information to parents or grandparents, who may not speak English.
- Providing, wherever possible, and where requested by the student, personal tutorship in which minority ethnic students were supported by minority ethnic staff.

However, while managers expressed enthusiasm and commitment towards these initiatives, they had not undertaken any systematic evaluation and were therefore unable to comment on their effectiveness.

Case study 3 was the most proactive in respect of attempting to increase the recruitment of minority ethnic students. Despite its programmes being heavily subscribed to, the college expressed a strong commitment towards maintaining a wide entry gate in order to maximize the opportunities available to prospective minority ethnic applicants. In part, this was in response to pressure from local NHS trusts, which were seeking to develop the ethnic profile of their workforce in order more accurately to reflect the ethnic mix of the local population. To this end, the college had worked closely with a local college of further education in establishing an access course specific-ally intended to facilitate people from minority ethnic communities who were interested in health professional careers to gain advanced GNVQs, which were recognized as equivalent to A level studies. However, the course was still in its infancy and it was as yet too early to gauge what the long-term demand for the course would be, together with its ultimate impact on minority ethnic recruitment.

The college also stressed the importance of influencing not just school leavers, but also younger children. As a result, it had established a number of links with leaders of local minority ethnic communities through whom it hoped to promote career opportunities in nursing. The college had also drawn upon the local council's inner city initiatives and, through working with the council's equal opportunities officer, had been able to disseminate information on education and job vacancies to a wide number of different groups and organizations. However, it was acknowledged that these initiat-ives were in the early stages of implementation and as yet it was too early to judge their effectiveness.

One of the main reasons why the case study 3 college appeared to be making some headway was in part because it had appointed a senior man-ager to take responsibility for recruitment, who expressed a strong personal commitment to addressing inequalities in all its forms. By contrast, the case study 2 college had lost its recruitment officer some 12 months before, on account of the rationalization of staff prior to integration with higher education. The remaining staff spoke of the hiatus that this created and the difficulties of trying to make progress in promoting the nursing profes-sions among minority ethnic communities. The case study 1 college had no such appointment, and this may help to explain something of its apparent inertia. That the one college which had earmarked a specific staff appoint-ment whose remit included promoting recruitment among minority ethnic communities appeared to be making the most progress suggests that this may be a beneficial strategy for institutions to adopt. But it may be worth noting that case study 3 was also the institution with the least coherent curricular response to preparing nurses to work in a multi-ethnic context. This should at least act as a reminder that addressing recruitment as solely an external activity beyond the college is a naive response, and one which may only later highlight the related challenge: that of retaining minority ethnic students after their entry onto the programme.

Conclusion

This stage of the study has served to highlight a number of issues associ-ated with the recruitment of students from minority ethnic backgrounds into the nursing professions, which merit further consideration. In particular, it identifies an urgent need for more accurate systems for monitoring the ethnic background of applicants to nursing and midwifery courses, both centrally and at an institution level, in order to monitor trends and form a basis for evaluating the effectiveness of recruitment strategies. It also highlights a somewhat fragmentary approach to promoting nursing and midwifery as career opportunities among the minority ethnic communities. Although there is evidence of a number of initiatives in the colleges, the effectiveness of these initiatives is not known, because either it is too early to form judgements or they have not been systematically evaluated. Clearly, if institutions are to make progress in increasing the representation from minority ethnic communities on their programmes, then these deficits need to be remedied.

7

Nursing for a multi-ethnic society: constructing the future

Introduction

In this chapter we wish to draw out some of the implications of the data we have presented in earlier chapters. In doing this we are fortunate that the differing elements of our research process have generated data which have cohered into a cumulative and consistent account. The findings from the national survey, while somewhat disappointing, were not inconsistent with the literature review we had carried out in preparing for our data collection. The data generated from the case studies have provided powerful exemplars of processes, practices and attitudes which are consistent with the broad framework provided by the national survey. The data reported in the case studies have been derived by a process of analysis carried out independently by colleagues who coded the focus group discussions, in relation to a methodology determined by the researchers. It is therefore reassuring that these data generate an account which is consistent with the researchers' experience of these locations. There is much in the shared personal experience of carrying out all the interviews and all the focus group discussions that has informed the research team in gaining a sense of the institutional culture in each location.

In the following pages we offer some of the insights which, we believe, may be legitimately derived from this research. The reader, with his or her own perspective and priorities, will have already identified key points of entry into the data. However, we wish to focus on three overarching areas of concern: issues associated with the curriculum, practice experience and the recruitment of people from minority ethnic communities into the nursing professions.

The curriculum

Our discussions of the insights we have gained starts with an examination of how different interested parties relate to the current curriculum. This rapidly leads to a necessary recognition of the context under which curricula are conceived and delivered. It is through acknowledging this context that a few ground rules are proposed for those of us who may be inclined to pursue curricular reform, whereupon some considerations for curriculum reform are presented.

It is apparent that the professional identity of students who have chosen one of the branches of nursing or midwifery may introduce a particular strain into the curriculum. The data from the case study revealed strong feelings about the relevance of the common foundation programme to those pursuing particular options as a career choice. The midwifery students in case study 2 and the mental health branch students in case study 3 shared some explicitly hostile views about the very limited relevance of the common foundation programme to their specialism. In each case they felt that they should have the distinct interests and specialist knowledge of their specialism introduced into the curriculum at the earliest possible point. This concern related to the substantive content of the taught programme and to the recognition of the specialist's practice priorities. For example, in case study 2 there had been some difficulties in the common foundation programme, where staff had tended to illustrate generic issues by reference to their own specialist practice experience, which was frequently adult nursing. This had been further compounded by personal tutors being required to tutor students across all the branches. This demand for the interests of the branch specialism to be anticipated in the common foundation programme is very probably a natural expression of strong professional in-group identities. However, it is also probably exacerbated by the widespread sense that the curriculum is under pressure to cover too much in too short a time; and consequently personal priorities for structuring the content of the curriculum tend to be strongly felt.

This is a view which was certainly apparent in the focus group discussions with staff and the interviews with managers. The apparently endless emergence of new topics which are articulated by interest groups, health authorities and/or the government are unwelcome to professional educationists struggling to sustain a coherent educational environment for students, when their own professional environment already seems to be characterized by frequent institutional merger and reorganization, and a reduction in their resource base. This being so, the commitment of some institutions to address the challenge of preparing students to work with minority ethnic clients is laudable. But as a general observation, it remains the case that those urging education institutions to respond to this professional demand must recognize that it is hardly a propitious moment to do so.

Regrettably, some institutions will invoke the unfortunate circumstances of the times, and their curriculum bursting at its seams, to resist such demands. And, of course, this line of resistance is all the more effective because it may be argued in the apparently reasonable discourse of resources and timetables. Hostility to the innovation in itself may never need to be declared. More sophisticated variants on this theme involve invoking the general fraught scenario, and then placing oneself and one's institution into a position of self-declared virtue by outlining an existing 'progressive' commitment. Whether it be in the area of disability, women's health or whatever, the implied claim is 'we have done our bit, ticked that box, we cannot reasonably be expected to do everything.' This is a strategy that is all the more powerful because not only may it serve as management rhetoric, it may also find support as a comforting crutch to individual staff who feel they cannot be expected to address yet another professional requirement. It then becomes a position that has institutional legitimacy.

Part of this perceived threat very often lies in a failure to take the time to clarify and understand what is being required. If it remains a massive, ambiguous and imminent threat then not surprisingly it has all the ingredients of a nightmare. A little reality testing is all that is needed to dispel such phantoms. In a multi-ethnic society, nursing and midwifery professionals must be competent to provide an equitable and appropriate service to all clients. This is reality, grounded in national demography, citizenship rights and professional self-respect. This is a professional expectation which requires innovation in individual practitioners' skills; but it is also the responsibility of government, health authorities, trusts and higher education institutions. Only nursing and midwifery professionals can deliver appropriate care to minority ethnic clients, but they are not solely responsible for its accomplishment. As previously discussed, there are structural and political forces which must also be responsive to the multi-ethnic identity of contemporary Britain. Perhaps if individual practitioners more loudly assert this reality they will be less likely to identify the challenge as solely personal, and consequently have more confidence in the reasonableness of finding that they may be struggling from recently declared unconscious incompetence towards sustained conscious competence. In case study 1 there was no complacent assertion that the college had fully equipped itself to prepare all students for a multi-ethnic clientele; but it had created a climate in which staff and students could confidently work towards that achievement.

Thus an initial requirement of any initiative to ensure that nursing and midwifery programmes of education adequately prepare practitioners to work with a multi-ethnic clientele must be an explicit recognition of the current constraints on professional education resulting from stretched resources and historical pressures to extend the curriculum. A logical corollary of this perspective is an acknowledgement that strategies to develop an appropriate curriculum must be accepted by all the interested parties currently shaping professional training. This is a task which requires integrated institutional responses. In the case studies there is ample evidence of tactical innovations in the curriculum which have not been adequately communicated to agencies providing the practice placements. Equally, there are examples of innovations within these agencies of which the college staff remain ignorant. This lack of managerial inter-agency collaboration is not only wasteful of resources, it also is unlikely to produce a coherent programme of innovation: the whole may well be less than the sum of the parts. Equally importantly, this piecemeal approach almost certainly dissipates the political will and commitment which has been generated around specific sites, and particular persons, within agencies and education institutions. The case studies revealed very clearly how particular individuals tend to be responsible for promoting transcultural competence as an issue in professional training. They also indicated how such individuals may be simultaneously marginalized and exploited. They are marginalized in that colleagues feel able to say that 'that's their bag – let them get on with it – my commitments lie elsewhere.' They are exploited in that these same colleagues, and the institutional management, are likely to invoke their 'good works' when asked to comment on how their programme addresses the needs of minority ethnic clients. Only a collective recognition of the challenge, and a collective ownership of the responsibility for the response, can provide a sound basis for developing a coherent learning experience for students.

This research has unambiguously supported Beishon *et al.*'s (1995) recent reporting of racism in the nursing professions, which is expressed verbally and behaviourally in the work place. This may certainly be expected to generate both explicit and subtle forms of resistance to strategies seeking to meet the needs of minority ethnic clients more appropriately. Nor is this resistance to be expected only in the practice setting, for the case studies have revealed the existence of similar sentiments among some students. Hostility to minority ethnic persons, and to investing in meeting their needs, must therefore be acknowledged as a factor to be faced in the development of professional training. Those responsible for professional development and practice standards in purchasing authorities, trusts and higher education institutions must clearly understand that the skills necessary to challenge racism in the practice context require specific professional education, and support through explicit institutional policy. The institutional and professional values which may be invoked in support of transcultural competencies may not adequately support attempts to challenge racism within institutional settings. Indeed, the individualism often inherent in legitimating transcultural competencies may help to obscure the institutional processes underpinning discriminating practices and racist oppression. Consequently, anti-oppressive policies must be explicit within institutional management structures. And personal confidence to invoke and implement these policies must be developed through professional training.

However, resistance is not only likely to be found in racist ideologies informing practitioners' beliefs and behaviour. The case studies have confirmed the expectations that might reasonably have been drawn from the national survey; namely that very many current practitioners are not adequately equipped to provide appropriate intercultural care to minority ethnic clients. As was discussed in Chapter 2, the experience of conscious incompetence is personally uncomfortable, and potentially professionally threatening. Herein lies the basis for an understandable anxiety when one is required to confront this area of practice as a professional necessity. Where this requirement is expressed bluntly, without explanation and without an understanding of the practitioners' professional development, this anxiety may be turned to resistance. A senior manager in case study 2 reported just such a response when an attempt to promote cultural awareness had been perceived by the practitioners as confrontational and condemnatory. A shotgun approach to cultural awareness and equal opportunities issues is not likely to be effective, and may well provide an opportunity for the participants to engage in a defensive collective confirmation of their own status as an oppressed majority.

It follows from this argument that a number of characteristics are required of attempts to develop professional education to enable practitioners to meet the needs of minority ethnic clients. They should start from a recognition of the current context of professional education and of the stresses inherent in it. They should anticipate the forms of resistance that are likely to develop as a response to any initiatives that might be proposed. They should be planned, coherent, inter-agency initiatives which draw upon unique strengths, rationalize resource costs and facilitate the sharing of a common framework for developments in training. Consequent upon the above, they must be unembarrassed by the political will which will have to be unambiguously evident so that such a programme may be accomplished. When majority institutions attempt to prioritize the needs of minority ethnic communities they have a habit of finding themselves being accused of being 'political'. It is regrettable that this has become a perceived slur. If Britain is to avoid the fracturing of the social fabric described in Galbraith's (1992) *The Culture of Contentment*, political participation is exactly what is needed in the contemporary social democracy. Given the socio-political profile of contemporary multi-ethnic Britain, 'being political' is a necessary characteristic of any who wish to shape social policy.

Fortunately, this research has in the case studies found evidence that there is a climate for change. As we noted in Chapter 1, health authorities and trusts are making an ability to work with a multi-ethnic clientele a specification within their contract setting; and colleges of nursing and higher education institutions are keen to be seen to be responding. One form of response detectable in the case studies is to begin to put in place an equal opportunity policy. Regrettably, while this may have implications for recruitment policies for staff and students, and establish internal procedures for the management of racial harassment, it may have little or no impact upon the curriculum. (Ambiguous properties of equal opportunity policies are discussed in Anthias and Yuval Davis 1993; Meekosha 1993). In case study 3 a senior manager spoke positively of the college's equal opportunity policy, but demonstrated real ambiguity as to how it reached into the curriculum. Consequently, care needs to be exercised lest an equal opportunity policy provides an institutional framework within which the curriculum and the manner of its delivery remain unquestioned and unchanged. One possible way of overcoming this problem is to seek to incorporate a minority ethnic perspective within the curriculum by involving minority ethnic users and representatives from community groups and organizations in curriculum development and programme management teams. The interviews with minority ethnic service users and representatives from community organizations which we presented in Chapter 3 help to focus a concern for practitioners not only to respond positively to ethnic diversity but also to acknowledge the effects of racism on minority ethnic experiences of health care. Such insights could be usefully and legitimately employed in the design, delivery and evaluation of educational programmes.

A definition of what would constitute the substantive content of an appropriate curriculum is not something which can reasonably be generated from this research project; but it has thrown up some useful insights. The data from the national survey in Chapter 4 indicated that all the subject areas in the curriculum had a demonstrable capacity to introduce issues relating to ethnic diversity and care in a multi-ethnic context into the students' learning. This is important, for it indicates that there is no inherent tendency for this area of practice to be relegated to one component of the programme, or to be hijacked as the monopoly interest of specific staff groups. The basis for ensuring a permeation of this issue throughout the curriculum is therefore structurally in place.

However, if permeation means only that the health care needs of minority ethnic communities and issues of ethnic diversity are routinely 'mentioned' in all programmes, this is hardly an optimum form of pedagogy. Permeation is a term which is often invoked to indicate a coherent pedagogic philosophy; and perhaps too often and too easily it provides a conceptual glue which holds together elements of an educational programme which are in fact *ad hoc* and a pragmatic expression of available resources. 'Permeation' is not a descriptive label which can be put on an educational programme retrospectively. If it means anything, it is as a framework for planning, and must start from a shared examination of what it would mean in the context of a specific educational context (see, for example, Shah 1989).

Much of what has been revealed in Chapters 4 and 5 relates to various forms of poor communication between educational staff, and between educational and practice personnel. Permeation requires not a peppering of all courses with fragments of relevant material, but a coherent integration of relevant information into a cumulative whole. This requires a degree of institutional coordination which, the national survey indicates, is far from usual. And it requires a dialogue between the education institution and practice which, this research suggests, is not currently in place. Putting in place this high-quality infrastructure is not a task which would uniquely benefit the preparation of students to work with a multi-ethnic clientele; it also would have generic benefits for the whole process of professional education.

The national survey in Chapter 4 indicated how significant was the contribution of teaching by lecturers from other institutions, and Chapter 5 has shown that teaching from other institutions may operate on a loose regulatory lead. Programmes may, because of contemporary pressure, find such styles of sharing education functionally adequate; but they are not desirable. Moreover, the case studies identified the tenuous links between the academic and practice placements, where again the level of communication was sufficient to sustain sharing a student, rather than meaningfully cooperating in shaping students' learning. As Chapter 4 demonstrated, relatively few programmes currently have identified a named member of staff with responsibility for overseeing the preparation of practitioners to meet the health care needs of minority ethnic clients. Such a post may, during the period of programmes developing their response to this need at least, be a necessity. It may also prove to be a great bonus in identifying untapped resources; since the research has indicated that innovation may be taking place in agencies which are unknown and untapped by education institutions.

This research has indicated how significant the local ethnic demography is in making education institutions aware of ethnic diversity as an unmistakable feature of the client population; and consequently inevitably relevant to their educational task. Equally, it has shown that some institutions feel able to report that, since ethnic diversity is not a significant feature of their locality, they have no need to address the issue. Demography is certainly relevant in pragmatically defining those minority ethnic communities that become the focus for developing cultural communicative competence, but no education institution can excuse itself from offering adequate intercultural training. Professional mobility alone makes this a necessity.

In Chapter 2 the distinction between cultural communicative competence and intercultural communicative competence was introduced as having a practical relevance to professional training. An example from case study 1 illustrates the point: 'I would imagine it's really hard to go into the nitty-gritty of every culture. And again I think what the educationalists can prepare you for is to give you a broad background as to what to expect, and how to be skilful at communicating and interpersonal skills' (1.4.8). This is a comment from a midwifery manager who had earlier spoken of her colleagues' familiarity with the local South Asian community's culture. She is making a point that was made by others in the case studies: namely, that developing competence in working with clients from particular cultures involves acquiring culturally specific knowledge that may not be appropriate in other practice settings. Thus students in areas of significant minority ethnic communities, as well as students in areas of predominantly majority ethnic communities, will benefit from being offered training in generic intercultural skills. Given a degree of hostility to minority ethnic clients among practitioners, revealed in this research, this would be a valuable activity, purely at the level of inhibiting the behavioural expression of negative feelings. But the intended relevance of intercultural competence lies in it providing a base line of transferable skills which will facilitate communication with clients from any culture. The holistic ethos of contemporary professional training is an entirely compatible framework for the acquisition of those skills which intercultural competence would expect to inculcate in practitioners.

At the same time, it must be noted that the case studies revealed a very clear demand from practitioners for information that would enable them to work more competently with specific minority ethnic communities. There is ample evidence of many practitioners in this study being aware of the dangers of stereotyping clients on the basis of the naive use of a little knowledge. And clearly there is a danger of students being given 'knowledge', without the understanding to render it relevant to practice. For this reason the practice experience is very highly valued by the students; for here book learning becomes existential learning. That practitioners and clients share experiences of care, from different perspectives, does not of course generate shared meanings. This was clearly indicated by the practitioners' comments about their difficulty of accepting what they 'knew' were the cultural norms of particular clients. Perhaps the nursing and midwifery professions might usefully reflect upon how their use of the concept of holistic care positions them, personally, as carers in relation to minority ethnic clients.

One aspect of the practitioners' experience of working with minority ethnic communities received considerable attention in the focus group discussions: this was language. Again and again difficulties in care were traced to a fundamental linguistic exclusion from communicating with the client. And, despite a number of agencies having in place link workers or interpreter services, these again were criticized as ineffective. One solution to this dilemma was identified in the recruitment of practitioners from the minority ethnic communities, who would speak the community language(s). This is certainly one appropriate strategy, but the nature of practice routines would be very radically changed indeed if it was assumed to be a sufficient solution to the problem. It became evident that some practitioners were taking instruction in the community languages, and others expressed a wish to do so. It would seem that there is another pressure on the curriculum. Certainly the professions should investigate means of facilitating language instruction for majority ethnic community practitioners. Essentially, this learning should be fully credited as professionally relevant training, not, as seems at present, an indication of a personal commitment. The data from our case studies also suggest that structurally the current provision and use of interpreter services is far from adequate and requires very careful evaluation and development.

The practice learning environment

The preceding consideration of the curriculum as a whole has served to highlight the significant role that practice experience plays in programmes of nursing and midwifery education. It forms an integral part of the overall learning experience that students engage in and provides an important medium through which they develop the requisite competencies to obtain their licence to practise as a nurse or midwife (ENB 1993). The potential importance of the practice learning environment in providing opportunities for students to develop the necessary intercultural and cultural competencies to practise in a multi-ethnic context has been emphasized throughout the different stages of the research. In particular, and as has previously been highlighted, students in each of the case study sites spoke very positively of the value derived from caring for minority ethnic clients and the contribution that this experience made to their understanding and application of knowledge to professional practice. However, the national survey also indicated that, with the exception of midwifery programmes, educationists expressed less confidence in the extent to which practice experience, as opposed to course work, equipped students with the necessary competencies to work in a multi-ethnic context. This anomaly can in part be explained by a consideration of some of the particularities of the nature and organization of practice experience within the overall curriculum. We therefore propose that there is a need to undertake a further and more detailed exploration of the practice learning environment. However, in doing so we would wish to emphasize that the intention of such an examination is to increase an understanding of education programmes as an integrated whole, and not to promote a view of the academic and practice components of curricula as separate and independent entities in their own right. Arguably, an enhanced understanding of the complexities of the learning which occurs in the practice setting can lead to a greater awareness of opportunities for curricular reform.

The data arising from both the survey and the case studies lead us to an observation that the practice placements which students undertake appear to exert both a defining and a confining influence on the nature and the quality of students' learning experiences. In particular, the characteristics of a specific placement have been seen to determine the learning opportunities available to the student and thus exert a considerable influence on what a student may learn during his or her time in that setting. As has been previously highlighted, the influence of local demography is key among these characteristics.

The need to focus teaching and learning on the perceived needs of local populations has been a recurring feature of this research, but this approach may have a potentially limiting effect on providing adequate opportunities for students to develop appropriate competencies to work in a multicultural context. The NHS reforms, most notably the 'purchaser–provider split', and the subsequent responsibility of health authorities to assess and make provision for health needs within their own catchment areas, appear to be a major factor contributing to this scenario. The concomitant reforms in nursing and midwifery education outlined in Chapter 1 have in turn required education institutions to be more responsive in preparing practitioners who are competent to meet the needs of local communities. This position was substantiated in each of the case study sites, where both education and service managers spoke of the need to equip nurses and midwives to be responsive to the local populations whom they served. However, this position places nursing and midwifery educators in the invidious position of educating practitioners to practise effectively in local situations, while at the same time recognizing the opportunities for and desirability of professional mobility. The issue here is that if education is limited according to the 'types' of clients student nurses and midwives may meet in practice settings, the significance of the meaning of professional registration as a national qualification is diluted. A *de facto* emphasis on cultural competence, with a resultant neglect of intercultural competence, must be resisted.

Local demography exerts a major influence on the learning opportunities available to students. The findings from the national survey indicated that, with the exception of midwifery, the majority of programmes were not able to provide practice placements specifically intended to provide students with the opportunity to develop intercultural and cultural competencies. Even where such placements were available, there appeared to be no guarantee that all students would be able to avail themselves of the opportunity to care for an ethnically diverse clientele. This observation was subsequently borne out in the three case study locations when participants in each of the student focus groups provided widely contrasting accounts of the opportunities they had encountered for caring for minority ethnic clients. While all students within a particular focus group were drawn from the same cohort, and therefore it might reasonably be expected that they would have encountered similar learning opportunities, the reality proved quite different. Some students spoke with considerable enthusiasm of enriching learning experiences, particularly as part of a community based placement, through which they had been exposed to caring for minority ethnic clients, whereas others within the same cohort had encountered minimal opportunities. This observation was initially somewhat surprising, bearing in mind the local demography of the cities in which the case study institutions were located. However, the interviews with education managers subsequently revealed some of the difficulties they encountered in managing placement allocations.

In many instances placements appeared to be organized around trust boundaries, with students undertaking much of their practice experience within a particular trust. The trusts in turn served particular sections of the local population determined largely by geographical boundaries. Thus, if a particular student was allocated to a trust which served an area in which there was a high minority ethnic population, then the student might reasonably expect to encounter minority ethnic clients on a number of different placements throughout the programme, whereas the converse was also true. This was aptly illustrated in case study 1 where, following the amalgamation of a number of smaller colleges of nursing and midwifery education over a period of some years, students were still allocated to

undertake the whole of their practice experience in a defined geographical location served by a particular trust which had previously been linked
to one of the smaller colleges. The anomaly in this institution, which may
well be present in others nationally, was that some students, in being denied the opportunity to avail themselves of the rich ethnically diverse local
population served by the college as a whole, failed to encounter minority
ethnic patients at all throughout their three-year programme. Invariably
this observation identifies both a need and an opportunity for institutions
to develop a more systematic approach to managing placement allocations
and, together with trusts, to develop a mutually beneficial approach towards
creating more flexible learning opportunities.

The research has also raised questions surrounding the importance placed
on local demography in defining the learning experiences of students required to develop skills to work effectively with Britain's multi-ethnic population. There is a concern that minority ethnic communities themselves
have become responsible for a large part of what is learnt by students, i.e.
that they become a critical learning resource. The confidence expressed by
participants throughout the case study investigations in the value of working with members of minority ethnic communities and caring for minority
ethnic clients may well demonstrate a growing respect for diversity. However, it is of concern that clients and their significant others, while made
vulnerable by the life event which caused them to become users of the
health service in the first place, should be taking a leading role in educating both students and clinical staff. There is an issue here of equity and
respect. Relying upon minority ethnic clients and carers as 'learning opportunities' is not the same as consciously incorporating their contribution
as teachers/mentors in the learning environment.

The issues raised above lead to a further important consideration. It
appears from the accounts of students that, although they benefit from
working directly with clients from different ethnic backgrounds, such
exposure does not guarantee effective learning. The availability of appropriate support to students during their practice experience is crucial and
raises questions regarding the role that nurse and midwife teachers might
play in assisting students to relate theory to practice by engaging more
actively in practice settings. The separation between college and practice
areas, highlighted in the case studies, indicates a lack of evidence of teachers
assuming an active role in monitoring the learning which takes place in
practice placements. Although teachers stressed that upon returning to
college following a placement experience, students would collectively evaluate their experiences, and this in turn provided a valuable learning opportunity, there was little evidence that teachers actively engaged in supporting
student learning in the practice setting. Rather, there appeared to be a
complacent expectation that all seemed to be going well, and that students
were developing appropriate transcultural competencies. In reality this
appears not to be so, given the reported experiences of being a witness to,
or personally experiencing, racist behaviour. As a result, students may find

themselves in the unhelpful position of working with minority ethnic clients and staff, yet acquiring skills in a discriminatory setting. Our often stated concern about the apparently minimal level of contact between education institutions and practice settings becomes a major issue when the context in which the student integrates theory and practice is considered. All education institutions need to develop close links with agencies which provide placements for their students, with teachers assuming a more proactive role in supporting student learning in practice settings (Gerrish 1992). Through such links, both teachers and mentors/assessors may develop a clearer understanding of their joint responsibilities towards their shared students, and have a more adequate understanding of the learning process, which currently is too often uniquely a property of the student.

In addition to this very real concern over the absence of a strong teaching presence in practice settings, there is the question of how effective mentors and assessors are in facilitating the development of intercultural and cultural competence in students. The fact that mentors and assessors often felt inadequately prepared to meet the needs of minority ethnic clients seriously brings into question their ability to support students' developing skills in this area and has implications for the continuing education opportunities made available to nurses and midwives. In each of the case study locations, mentors and assessors made reference to the fact that they learnt from the students they were supporting. Although this willingness to be open about sharing knowledge is commendable, it does raise questions about the ability of practitioners to assess students in this area. It has been suggested by a small number of participants that students are not being assessed in intercultural and cultural competence; instead, objectives are simply being 'ticked' by assessors who are uncomfortably aware of their own lack of understanding. This level of honesty and openness proffered by participants suggests that they experience very real anxiety in this area. We would advocate that a sympathetic understanding of the pressures placed on mentors must be a vital consideration in determining a strategy for a more supportive and communicative relationship between academic and practice-based staff. As clearly demonstrated in the presentation of the findings from the case studies, the importance of clear and reflexive cooperation between academic and practice areas cannot be too highly prized. Case study 1 is an exemplar of such an achievement, and despite its having the advantage of being the smallest centre in the study, the levels of cooperation and relationship building at both individual and institutional levels are capable of being replicated elsewhere.

The research has also shown that the integration of theory and practice, while advanced at a conceptual level, is seldom reflected in the assessment process. The national survey indicated that very few institutions incorporated explicit learning outcomes relating to providing care within a multi-ethnic context within the assessment requirements for practice placements. Consequently, there was no guarantee that students would be assessed in this area. If students are to develop the ability to function effectively in a multi-ethnic society, it follows that practice experiences need not only to provide them with the opportunity to apply relevant knowledge to caring for clients from different ethnic communities, but also to ensure that their developing competencies are formally assessed. This should include not only their ability to provide ethnically sensitive care but also a recognition of the effects of racism on minority ethnic clients' experiences of health and health care and the development of appropriate anti-oppressive practices. Although such skills may be demonstrated most effectively by students providing direct care to minority ethnic clients, we would suggest that, irrespective of the presence of minority ethnic clients, students should still be able to demonstrate a sensitivity towards difference, disadvantage and discrimination, whether it is manifest through race, gender, age, class or disability. Such sensitivity is then transferable to other contexts that students may encounter in the future.

Recruitment issues

In Chapter 6 we presented our analysis of the part of the study which examined issues associated with the recruitment of minority ethnic students into nursing and midwifery education. In view of the extremely limited national data that were available to us on the ethnic background of applicants to nursing and midwifery programmes of education, the conclusions which can be drawn from the findings of this stage are inevitably more tentative. Nevertheless, they do provide some important indicators for future development. In particular, there is an urgent need for more accurate systems to be established for monitoring the ethnic background of applicants to nursing and midwifery programmes in order to monitor trends over a period of time.

The data presented in Chapter 6 have indicated that while the percentage of minority ethnic students undertaking nursing and midwifery education collectively approximates to that of the general population, they are disproportionately over-represented in mental health nursing in comparison to adult nursing and midwifery. In addition, 'Black' minority groups are over-represented in proportion to 'Asian' ethnic minorities. The findings also suggest that minority ethnic applicants are less likely to secure a place on nursing and midwifery programmes than white applicants. However, as we have previously pointed out, the limitations of current ethnic monitoring systems present a number of difficulties in the accurate interpretation of ethnic data, not least the very real problem in the first place of relying on the current approach to ethnic classification. We also recognize that identifying ethnic origin on application is not a current requirement, and as the data have indicated, 14 per cent of applicants chose not to identify their ethnic origin at the time of application. That these applicants, should they secure a place, may subsequently declare their ethnicity on indexing with the ENB at the commencement of the programme inevitably affects the accuracy with which interpretations can be made on the success of applicants from different ethnic backgrounds. Notwithstanding these limitations, there is a need to examine in more detail why minority ethnic applicants are seemingly less successful than white applicants in securing places on nursing and midwifery programmes. This is particularly pertinent bearing in mind the discrimination reported by qualified minority ethnic nurses pursuing career opportunities in Beishon *et al.*'s (1995) study. One of the influencing factors noted above may be the proportion of overseas applicants, and this is an issue which merits further consideration. A major limitation of the current data is that there are no means of differentiating between overseas and UK citizens. Monitoring systems therefore need to be developed to identify more accurately those applicants who are UK citizens and those from overseas.

The present system of monitoring the ethnic background of applicants and those who subsequently commence a programme of nursing or midwifery education is a welcome recent initiative. However, in view of the North American literature which indicated higher attrition rates among minority ethnic students, there is a need to extend the monitoring procedures to include ethnicity as a variable in respect of attrition and completion rates. Other reports have highlighted the high attrition rates from Project 2000 nursing programmes (National Audit Office 1992); however, the ethnicity of students leaving programmes has not been recorded. None of the colleges we visited had systems in place for monitoring the ethnic background of those withdrawing from programmes. Although one college had instigated a process of exit interviews with students who left before completing the programme in order to ascertain their reasons for withdrawal, there was no indication that this information was used in any systematic way to improve retention rates. Unless these data are collected, it will not be possible to identify the appropriate support required by minority ethnic students undertaking nursing and midwifery programmes. Certainly, the experiences of minority ethnic students in social work professional training points to the need for institutions of education to consciously examine how user-friendly their curricula and physical environment are to minority ethnic students, and to plan for their support (de Souza 1991).

The three case study institutions all voiced a concern to increase the recruitment of students from minority ethnic communities to reflect more accurately the ethnic mix of local populations. However, they had made little in the way of real progress in realizing their intentions. Although they postulated a number of reasons as to why recruitment was poor, few of their marketing and recruitment practices were targeted specifically at minority ethnic communities. Two of the colleges were making some early progress in attempting to overcome these difficulties; the remaining one appeared to exhibit a degree of complacency in promoting nursing and midwifery as career options among minority ethnic populations. This is of particular concern, bearing in mind the ethnic diversity of local populations in the vicinity of the case study sites. The interviews with education and service managers indicated limited insight into the issues which might influence recruitment of students from minority ethnic groups, and reflected stereotypical images of minority ethnic communities which were largely unsubstantiated. Furthermore, none of them had sought to establish close links with local minority ethnic communities in order to promote the nursing professions as career options, although the case study 3 institution had recently received some funding from the Department of Health to undertake work in this area. The very limited evidence of coherent organizational planning between education and service managers suggests that some possible initiatives across institutional boundaries are unlikely to be conceived of or implemented. The difficulty with the current situation is that recruitment strategies are based on the educationists' perceptions of the most effective means of recruiting minority ethnic students and may well be misinformed. There is clearly a need for further research which seeks to ascertain the perceptions of minority ethnic communities as to the appropriateness of nursing or midwifery as careers in order to target recruitment strategies more effectively.

However, the recruitment of minority ethnic students should not be viewed in isolation from the environment in which students find themselves undertaking nursing and midwifery education, and brings to the fore a consideration of the effects of racism on the student experience. This is an important issue to consider for all students, irrespective of their ethnicity, but it is particularly salient in respect of minority ethnic students. Although there is a need to address the problem of racism through the monitoring of equal opportunity policies, the data arising from the case studies have raised a number of additional considerations. Participants in each of the different focus groups acknowledged the existence of racism in both the college and practice settings. That teachers in each of the case study sites felt ill-equipped to challenge racist sentiments expressed in classroom settings brings into question their ability to support minority ethnic students who may be subject to racial prejudice and leaves the minority ethnic student in a particularly vulnerable and unsupported position. The North American literature suggests that there may be benefits to providing specific counselling and pastoral support for minority ethnic students (Jones 1992; Kavanagh et al. 1993). Although in the second case study site there was an attempt to provide minority ethnic students with a personal tutor who was also from a minority ethnic background if the students so wished, this provision had not been monitored and evaluated. We would suggest that this is an area which merits further consideration in both initial and in-service teacher education programmes.

The racism that students are exposed to in practice settings is more difficult to address and requires further investigation. The problems that both students and qualified staff experienced in responding to racism expressed by clients is supported by Beishon et al. (1995) and raises important issues regarding how racial harassment can be addressed most effectively. We would suggest two key areas for future consideration. First, there is a need for an anti-oppressive dimension to be built into not just pre-registration curricula but also continuing education programmes, in order to ensure that practitioners are competent at challenging racist behaviours. Second, these issues underline the need for much closer cooperation between education institutions and practice settings in developing equal opportunities and anti-oppressive strategies in an inter-agency context of health care delivery. This might, among other things, include the adoption of a formal policy proscribing verbal and behavioural expressions of xenophobia and racism, applicable to all staff and clients, with appropriate mechanisms for its enforcement.

Finally, the data arising from the case studies have brought to our attention the need to consider the position that minority ethnic students and staff occupy within education institutions and the health services. In particular, there was a tendency for minority ethnic students to be invoked as experts in matters relating to ethnicity and to be made a critical resource in relation to the learning of fellow students and staff. This places a considerable and unreasonable burden on minority ethnic students and detracts from the need for such students themselves to develop the skills to work in a multi-ethnic society, which importantly for some may include the white majority population. It also fails to take account of the fact that second and third generation British minority communities occupy a complex cultural space; and expectations made about their ability or willingness to represent different ethnic perspectives should not be unthinkingly imposed. However, this is not to say that minority ethnic students do not have a particular contribution to make, but rather that there is a need for programme teams to consider how their experiences may be genuinely valued, and validated, within the educational institutions.

Focus group participants in each of the case study sites made very positive statements about the distinct contribution that minority ethnic staff make in terms of cultural competence. The students in particular placed emphasis on the value of working alongside a mentor who was from the same minority ethnic background as the clients for whom they were caring. The insights into and understandings of responding to ethnic diversity that this experience gave the students were considered some of the most valuable learning opportunities for equipping them with the skills to meet the needs of minority ethnic clients. However, the point that we would wish to make is that there is a potential danger for minority ethnic staff in this exposed position. First, and in the light of the points we have made above about racism, we must acknowledge the irony that a collectivity of persons who have experiences of discrimination and marginalization within the professions should find themselves so valued. One danger that has been suggested by the data is the displacement on to minority ethnic persons of the responsibility for providing expertise on minority ethnic issues. There is a risk that minority ethnic staff and students may be made professional *idiots savants*, uniquely knowledgeable only on matters of ethnicity. They are then in an invidious position of acting as a buffer between the needs of minority ethnic communities and the service context of essentially white institutions. Not only does this disempower minority ethnic staff and students; the case studies have also indicated that it provides white teachers and managers with the opportunity to deny responsibility for developing appropriate cultural competence.

The case studies have indicated that there is a danger that minority ethnic students and staff are seen chiefly as a means of solving particular difficulties encountered in caring for minority ethnic clients, the most notable of these being the difficulties of communication. There appeared to be an assumption that minority ethnic practitioners would speak the same language as clients, but this was not always the case, and where they did speak the same language there was a very real danger that their role was reduced to being that of interpreter. Indeed, one white student spoke with considerable concern about another student within her cohort who was fluent in one of the local community languages and who had spent a considerable amount of time on a placement acting as an interpreter. This serves to illustrate the potentially vulnerable position that minority ethnic students may occupy, and highlights the need to look beyond the objective of increasing recruitment from minority ethnic communities to the nature of support required by minority ethnic students, in order to ensure that they have a meaningful learning experience which develops in them the ability to practise effectively in a multi-ethnic society. They too need to develop intercultural competence.

Conclusion

In the course of carrying out the research, the research team has encountered professionals with commitment to and enthusiasm for developing the curriculum, in order better to prepare students to work in a multi-ethnic society. Within and beyond the case studies, there are examples of innovation in educational institutions and in practice settings. On the other hand, our national survey suggests that the professional training of nurses and midwives is, in the majority of institutions, just beginning to address how adequately their curricula are suited to prepare practitioners for working with a multi-ethnic clientele. Our argument here has been that this requires both an individual and an institutional commitment to change.

Although the primary aim of the research study was to undertake an in-depth examination of nursing and midwifery curricula in order to form some judgement as to the extent to which practitioners are prepared through their pre-registration programmes of education to meet the health care needs of minority ethnic communities, we were aware from the very outset of the importance of taking cognizance of the broader context in which nursing and midwifery education takes place. This concern was borne out through each of the different stages of the research, as the participants brought to our attention the complex and wide ranging factors which impact upon the preparation of practitioners to function effectively in a multi-ethnic society. While some of the issues which arise from the research may readily be addressed by those directly involved in curriculum delivery, others have more far-reaching implications and require changes in policy as well as practice.

If there is an overall conclusion of the study it is hardly surprising: namely, that although there is a general sense that many programmes have begun to address the issue of how to prepare practitioners to work in a multi-ethnic society, there is still much to be achieved. The current position is not one which those involved in nursing and midwifery education should be content to defend as an adequate preparation for professional practice; neither is it able to assure potential employees that they are producing staff who are competent to practise in a multi-ethnic society. However, it is encouraging that there are examples of innovation and good practice which can be built upon. While much of the responsibility for taking this work forward resides with those directly involved in education provision, it cannot be their responsibility alone. Achieving the effective preparation of practitioners for a multi-ethnic society requires the commitment and active involvement of a number of parties. In returning to the contextual issues which informed our thinking at the outset of the study, and which we highlighted in Chapter 1, we readily acknowledge the role that education commissioners, health service purchasers and providers and statutory professional bodies will increasingly play in shaping the future direction of nursing and midwifery education. It behoves these various parties to share a collective responsibility for ensuring that pre-registration programmes of nursing and midwifery education do achieve the intention of equipping practitioners with the necessary competencies to meet the health care needs of minority ethnic communities.

Appendix 1

BRADFORD AND AIREDALE COLLEGE OF HEALTH
and
THE UNIVERSITY OF BRADFORD

THE PREPARATION OF PRACTITIONERS TO MEET THE HEALTH
CARE NEEDS OF ETHNIC MINORITY GROUPS

Questionnaire

Common Foundation Programme

Please answer all questions by ticking the appropriate boxes and adding comments as requested.

1 When did your institution first start to offer a pre-registration diploma programme leading to Parts 12 and 13 (adult and mental health nursing) of the professional register?

   Month _____   Year _____

2 We are interested in identifying which broad areas of study within the curriculum are important in enabling nurses to acquire the knowledge base needed to deliver care which is sensitive to the health care needs of ethnic minorities.

   Could you please identify those broad areas of study, for example, sociology, or nursing theory, within the common foundation programme curriculum which provide this knowledge base.

   a _____
   b _____
   c _____

d _____

e _____

f _____

g _____

h _____

i _____

j _____

3   For each of the areas of study identified in question 2, please indicate who, from the following categories, are responsible for teaching students to meet the health care needs of ethnic minorities. Please tick one or more boxes as appropriate.

	Nursing lecturers from the approved institution	*Non nursing lecturers from the approved institution*	*Lecturers from other education institutions*	*Practitioners from health care settings*	*Members of ethnic minorities drawn from the community*
_____	☐	☐	☐	☐	☐
_____	☐	☐	☐	☐	☐
_____	☐	☐	☐	☐	☐
_____	☐	☐	☐	☐	☐
_____	☐	☐	☐	☐	☐
_____	☐	☐	☐	☐	☐
_____	☐	☐	☐	☐	☐
_____	☐	☐	☐	☐	☐
_____	☐	☐	☐	☐	☐
_____	☐	☐	☐	☐	☐
_____	☐	☐	☐	☐	☐

4   Different strategies may be employed in preparing practitioners to meet the health care needs of ethnic minorities, such as permeation of the whole curriculum, the provision of specific modules/units, or other strategies. Please briefly describe the approaches taken within your curriculum.

_____

_____

_____

_____

_____

_____

_____

_____

_____

_____

_____

_____

5 Some of the topics identified below may be included in the common foundation programme curriculum. If they are, please indicate the extent to which they feature.

	Not included	Briefly mentioned	Introduced and given some attention	Given extensive coverage
Concepts of ethnicity, culture and race	☐	☐	☐	☐
Health beliefs relevant to different ethnic minorities	☐	☐	☐	☐
Ethnic minorities' health needs	☐	☐	☐	☐
Ethnic minorities' access to health services	☐	☐	☐	☐
The social and political contexts of ethnic minorities' health	☐	☐	☐	☐
The social and political contexts of ethnic minorities' health care provision	☐	☐	☐	☐
Legislative implications for health care provision for ethnic minorities	☐	☐	☐	☐
Biological determinants influencing ethnic minorities' health	☐	☐	☐	☐
Activities of daily living within different cultures	☐	☐	☐	☐
Culturally appropriate assessment and identification of need	☐	☐	☐	☐
Intercultural communication	☐	☐	☐	☐
Transcultural nursing	☐	☐	☐	☐

6   Please identify any topics, additional to those listed in question 5, that are included in the common foundation programme curriculum specifically to assist in the preparation of practitioners to meet the health care needs of ethnic minorities.

	Briefly mentioned	*Introduced and given some attention*	*Given extensive coverage*
_____	☐	☐	☐
_____	☐	☐	☐
_____	☐	☐	☐
_____	☐	☐	☐
_____	☐	☐	☐

7   Do students have the opportunity to undertake a detailed study of a client/client group from a different culture to their own as part of the common foundation programme?

Yes   No
☐   ☐

If yes, please give a brief description of the type(s) of study.

8 We are interested in any innovative teaching and learning strategies used to deliver the components of the curriculum which prepare nurses to meet the health care needs of ethnic minorities. Please identify the subject/topic, for example, language barriers in communication, and provide a brief description of the teaching/learning strategies employed.

Example 1

_____
_____
_____
_____
_____
_____
_____
_____
_____
_____
_____
_____

Example 2

_____
_____
_____
_____
_____
_____
_____
_____
_____
_____

9 Please identify any specific texts, together with their authors, which are used to deliver the components of the common foundation programme curriculum that prepare nurses to meet the health care needs of ethnic minorities. (You may prefer to append the relevant course reading lists.)

_____
_____
_____
_____
_____
_____

10 Is there a named person(s) with specific responsibility for overseeing the preparation of nurses to meet the health care needs of ethnic minorities?

Yes   No
□   □

If yes, please give their title(s) and provide a brief description of their role within the course.

_____
_____
_____
_____
_____
_____
_____
_____

11 Have any individual members of teaching staff undergone specific staff development to prepare them to deliver the ethnic related aspects of the curriculum?

Yes   No
□   □

If yes, please give details.

_____
_____
_____
_____
_____
_____

12 Do the learning outcomes/objectives for practice placements in the common foundation programme make explicit reference to meeting the needs of clients from ethnic minorities, or is it implicit within more general statements of learning outcomes; for example, those that refer to 'individualized care'?

Explicit reference   Implicit reference
□   □

13 Are there any practice placements within the common foundation programme which are specifically intended to offer an opportunity for students to develop care sensitive to the needs of ethnic minorities?

Yes   No
☐   ☐

If yes, please provide details.

_____

_____

_____

_____

_____

_____

Are all students provided with an opportunity to undertake such a
placement?

Yes   No
☐   ☐

14 To what extent do you think that students are sufficiently prepared through
their course work and practice placements to successfully meet the health
care needs of ethnic minority clients in their practice?

Course work.

_____

_____

_____

_____

_____

_____

_____

_____

_____

_____

_____

_____

Practice placements.

_____

_____

_____

_____

_____

_____

_____

_____

_____

_____

_____

_____

15   There may be issues that we have not given you the opportunity to com-
     ment on. Please provide any additional information which you think may
     be helpful.

_____

_____

_____

_____

_____

_____

_____

_____

_____

_____

_____

_____

_____

_____

_____

_____

_____

_____

_____

_____

_____

Thank you for your assistance in completing this questionnaire.

Appendix 2

Focus group agenda (teachers)

1 In what ways is a concern with the health care needs of ethnic minorities made an issue in this programme?
2 In relation to the programme, what do you see as its particular strengths in preparing practitioners to meet the health care needs of minority ethnic clients? Perhaps you might like to give some examples in relation to the theoretical component and professional practice.
3 Could we now move on to discuss some of the difficulties you have encountered in addressing the health care needs of minority ethnic clients within your teaching of students?
4 You have discussed some of the difficulties. Perhaps now you might like to consider the limitations of what you have achieved in this area.
5 What ideas have you got for how the programme could be further developed?
6 How adequately do you feel you have been prepared for your role in teaching students to meet the needs of minority ethnic clients?
7 Thinking about practitioners in general, how adequately do you feel they are equipped to meet the needs of minority ethnic clients?
8 Are there any other issues that we have not discussed which you think are important?

References

Afshar, H. (1994) Muslim women in West Yorkshire, in H. Afshar and M. Maynard (eds) *The Dynamics of 'Race' and Gender*. London: Taylor and Francis.

Ahmad, W.I.U. (1992a) The maligned health: the 'hakim' and western medicine, *New Community*, 18(4), 521–36.

Ahmad, W.I.U. (1992b) 'Race' disadvantage and discourse: contextualising Black people's health, in W.I.U. Ahmad (ed.) *The Politics of Race and Health*. Bradford: University of Bradford and Bradford and Ilkley Community College, Race Relations Research Unit.

Ahmad, W.I.U. (ed.) (1993a) *'Race' and Health in Contemporary Britain*. Buckingham: Open University Press.

Ahmad, W.I.U. (1993b) Making black people sick: 'race', ideology and health research, in W.I.U. Ahmad (ed.) *'Race' and Health in Contemporary Britain*. Buckingham: Open University Press.

Ahmad, W.I.U. (1996) Consanguinity and related demons: science and racism in the debate on consanguinity and birth outcome, in N. South and C. Sampson (eds) *Constructing Social Policy*. Basingstoke: Macmillan.

Ahmad, W.I.U. and Husband, C. (1993) Religious identity, citizenship and welfare: the case of Muslims in Britain, *American Journal of Islamic Social Sciences*, 10(3), 217–33.

Ahmad, W.I.U., Kernohan, E.E.M. and Baker, M.R. (1989) Patients' choice of general practitioner: influence of patients' fluency in English and the ethnicity and sex of doctor, *Journal of Royal College of General Practitioners*, 39, 153–5.

Ahmad, W.I.U. and Walker, R. (1996) Health and social care needs of Asian older people, *Aging and Society*, in the press.

Akinsanya, J. (1988) Ethnic minority nurses, midwives and health visitors: what role for them in the National Health Service?, *New Community*, 14, 444–50.

Allport, G.W. (1954) *The Nature of Prejudice*. Reading, MA: Addison-Wesley.

Alvarez, A. and Abriam-Yago, K. (1993) Mentoring undergraduate ethnic minority students: a strategy for retention, *Journal of Nursing Education*, 32, 230–2.

Anderson, B. (1991) *Imagined Communities*. London: Verso.

Anionwu, E.N. (1993) Sickle cell and thalassaemia: community experiences and official response, in W.I.U. Ahmad (ed.) *'Race' and Health in Contemporary Britain*. Buckingham: Open University Press.

Anthias, F. and Yuval-Davis, N. (1993) *Racialized Boundaries*. London: Routledge.

Applegate, J. and Sypher, H. (1988) A constructivist theory of communication and culture, in Y. Kim and W. Gudykunst (eds) *Theories in Intercultural Communication*. Newbury Park, CA: Sage.

Argyle, M. (1975) *Bodily Communication*. London: Methuen.

Aspinall, P.J. (1995) Department of Health's requirement for mandatory collection of data on ethnic group of inpatients, *British Medical Journal*, 311, 1006–9.

Balarajan, R. and Bulusu, L. (1990) Mortality among immigrants in England and Wales, in M. Britton (ed.) *Mortality and Geography: a Review of the Mid-1980s*. London: OPCS.

Balarajan, R. and Raleigh, V. (1993) *Ethnicity and Health: a Guide for the NHS*. London: Department of Health.

Baldwin, D. and Wold, J. (1993) Students from disadvantaged backgrounds: satisfaction with a mentor-protégé relationship, *Journal of Nursing Education*, 32, 225–6.

Banton, M. and Harwood, J. (1975) *The Race Concept*. Newton Abbott: David and Charles.

Barker, M. (1981) *The New Racism*. London: Junction Books.

Barth, F. (1969) *Ethnic Groups and Boundaries*. Bergen: Universitetsforlaget.

Bauman, Z. (1990) Modernity and ambivalence, in M. Featherstone (ed.) *Global Culture*. London: Sage.

Baxter, C. (1988) *The Black Nurse: an Endangered Species. A Case for Equal Opportunities in Nursing*. London: National Extension College.

Beishon, S., Virdee, S. and Hagell, A. (1995) *Nursing in a Multi-ethnic NHS*. London: Policy Studies Institute.

Benezeval, M., Judge, K. and Solomon, M. (1992) *The Health Status of Londoners: a Comparative Approach*. London: King's Fund.

Bharj, K.K. (1995) *Nurse Recruitment: an Asian Response*. Bradford: Race Relations Research Unit, University of Bradford and Bradford and Ilkley Community College.

Bhavnani, K. and Pheonix, A. (1994) Shifting identities, shifting racisms, *Feminism and Psychology*, 4(1), 5–18.

Blakemore, K. and Boneham, M. (1994) *Age, Race and Ethnicity*. Buckingham: Open University Press.

Block, B. and Monroy, L. (eds) (1983) *Ethnic Nursing Care: a Multicultural Approach*. St Louis: Mosby.

Bottomore, T. (1992) Citizenship and social class, forty years on, in T.H. Marshall and T. Bottomore (eds) *Citizenship and Social Class*. London: Pluto Press.

Bourne, J. (1980) Cheerleaders and ombudsmen: the sociology of race relations in Britain, *Race and Class*, 21(4), 331–52.

Brewer, M. and Campbell, D. (1976) *Ethnocentrism and Intergroup Attitudes*. New York: John Wiley.

Bryan, B., Dadzie, S. and Scafe, S. (1985) *The Heart of the Race*. London: Virago.

Burkitt, I. (1991) *Social Selves*. London: Sage.

Butler, G.A. (1993) Racial equality in nursing and midwifery education: myth or reality, unpublished MA dissertation, University of Lancaster.

Byerly, E. (1977) Cultural components in the baccalaureate nursing curriculum:

philosophy, goals and processes, in National League for Nurses, *Cultural Dimensions in the Baccalaureate Nursing Curriculum: Workshop Papers*. New York: National League for Nurses.

Cassidy, J. (1995) Ethnic dilemma, *Nursing Times*, 91, 18.

CCETSW (1991a) *Setting the Context for Change: Anti-racist Social Work Education*. London: Central Council for Education and Training in Social Work.

CCETSW (1991b) *One Small Step towards Racial Justice*. London: Central Council for Education and Training in Social Work.

CCETSW (1992) *Anti-racist Social Work Education: Six Training Manuals*. London: Central Council for Education and Training in Social Work.

Centre for Contemporary Cultural Studies (1982) *The Empire Strikes Back*. London: Hutchinson.

Centre for Reviews and Dissemination (1996) *Ethnicity and Health: Reviews of Literature and Guidance for Purchasers in the Areas of Cardiovascular Disease, Mental Health and Haemoglobinopathies*. York: NHS Centre for Reviews and Dissemination.

Colley, L. (1992) *Britons: Forging the Nation*. New Haven, CT: Yale University Press.

Commission for Racial Equality (1984) *Race Relations Code of Practice for the Elimination of Racial Discrimination and the Promotion of Equality of Opportunity in Employment*. London: Commission for Racial Equality.

Commission for Racial Equality (1989) *Race Relations Code of Practice for the Elimination of Racial Discrimination and the Promotion of Equality of Opportunity in Education*. London: Commission for Racial Equality.

Commission for Racial Equality (1992) *Race Relations Code of Practice in Primary Health Care Services for the Elimination of Racial Discrimination and the Promotion of Equality of Opportunities*. London: Commission for Racial Equality.

Commission for Racial Equality (1994) *Race Relations Code of Practice in Maternity Services for the Elimination of Racial Discrimination and the Promotion of Equality of Opportunities*. London: Commission for Racial Equality.

Culley, L. (1996) A critique of multiculturalism in health care: the challenge for nurse education, *Journal of Advanced Nursing*, 23, 564–70.

Curtis, L.P. (1968) *Anglo-Saxons and Celts*. New York: New York University Press.

Curtis, L.P. (1971) *Apes and Angels: the Irishman in Victorian Caricature*. Newton Abbott: David and Charles.

Danziger, K. (1976) *Interpersonal Communication*. Oxford: Pergamon.

Day, M. (1994) Racial discrimination: professional implications, *Journal of Interprofessional Care*, 8(2), 135–40.

Department of Health (1989a) *Working for Patients*. London: HMSO.

Department of Health (1989b) *Caring for People: Community Care in the Next Decade and Beyond*. London: HMSO.

Department of Health (1989c) *Working for Patients: Education and Training, Working Paper 10*. London: HMSO.

Department of Health (1991) *The Patient's Charter: Raising the Standard*. London: HMSO.

Department of Health (1992) *The Health of the Nation: a Strategy for Health in England*. London: HMSO.

Department of Health (1993a) *Ethnicity and Health: a Guide for the NHS*. London: Department of Health.

Department of Health (1993b) *Ethnic Minority Staff in the NHS: a Programme of Action.* London: NHSME.

Department of Health (1995a) *On the State of the Public Health for the Year 1994.* London: HMSO.

Department of Health (1995b) *Variations in Health.* London: Department of Health.

DeSantis, L. (1994) Making anthropology clinically relevant to nursing care, *Journal of Advanced Nursing*, 20, 707–15.

De Souza, P. (1991) A review of the experiences of black students in social work training, in CCETSW, *One Small Step towards Racial Justice.* London: Central Council for Education and Training in Social Work.

de Vaus, D.A. (1985) *Surveys in Social Research*, 3rd edn. London: Allen & Unwin.

Dobson, S. (1986) Ethnography: a tool for learning, *Nurse Education Today*, 6, 76–9.

Dobson, S. (1992) *Transcultural Nursing: a Contemporary Imperative.* London: Scutari Press.

Douglas, M. (1973) *Natural Symbols.* Harmondsworth: Penguin.

English National Board (1989) *Project 2000 – 'A New Preparation for Practice'. Guidelines and Criteria for Course Development and the Formation of Collaborative Links between Approved Training Institutions and within the NHS and Centres of Higher Education.* London: English National Board.

English National Board (1993) *Regulations and Guidelines for the Approval of Institutions and Courses.* London: English National Board.

Esmail, E. and Everington, S. (1993) Racial discrimination against doctors from ethnic minorities, *British Medical Journal*, 306, 691–2.

Essed, P. (1991) *Understanding Everyday Racism.* London: Sage.

Fernando, S. (1991) *Mental Health, Race and Culture.* Basingstoke: Macmillan.

Foot, P. (1965) *Immigration and Race in British Politics.* Harmondsworth: Penguin.

Fryer, P. (1984) *Staying Power: the History of Black People in Britain.* London: Pluto Press.

Fulton, C. (1985) Integrating cultural content into the nursing curriculum, *Nurse Educator*, 10(1), 26–31.

Furnham, A. and Bochner, S. (1986) *Culture Shock.* London: Routledge.

Galbraith, J.K. (1992) *The Culture of Contentment.* London: Sinclair-Stevenson.

Geipel, J. (1969) *The Europeans: an Ethnohistorical Survey.* London: Longman.

Gerrish, K. (1992) The nurse teacher's role in the practice setting, *Nurse Education Today*, 12, 227–32.

Gilroy, P. (1990) The end of anti-racism, in W. Ball and J. Solomos (eds) *Race and Local Politics.* London: Macmillan.

Goldberg, D.T. (1994) *Multiculturalism: a Critical Reader.* Oxford: Blackwell.

Gordon, P. (1990) A dirty war: the New Right and local authority anti-racism, in W. Ball and J. Solomos (eds) *Race and Local Politics.* London: Macmillan.

Gudykunst, W. (1988) *Intergroup Communication.* Clevedon: Multilingual Matters.

Gurnah, A. (1989) The politics of racism awareness training, *Critical Social Policy*, 10, Winter, 6–24.

Hall, E.T. (1959) *The Silent Language.* New York: Doubleday.

Hall, E.T. (1966) *The Hidden Dimension.* Garden City, NY: Doubleday.

Harris, M. (1977) *Cannibals and Kings.* Glasgow: William Collins.

Hechter, M. (1975) *Internal Colonialism.* London: Routledge and Kegan Paul.

Hilbourne, J., Powell, A. and Fields, H. (1994) Improving the effectiveness of quality assurance systems in health care education and training: report of a workshop attended by WP10 'leads', 1–2 November 1993. HEQC, NHS Management Executive, Yorkshire Health.

Hobsbawm, E.J. and Ranger, T. (eds) (1983) *The Invention of Tradition*. Cambridge: Cambridge University Press.

Hollin, C.R. and Trower, P. (1986) *Handbook of Social Skills Training*. Oxford: Pergamon Press.

Holmes, C. (1978) *Immigrants and Minorities in British Society*. London: George Allen & Unwin.

hooks, b. (1991) *Yearning, Yearning*. London: Turnaround Press.

Howell, W. (1982) *The Empathic Communicator*. Belmont, CA: Wadsworth.

Humphrey, D. and John, G. (1971) *Because They're Black*. Harmondsworth: Penguin.

Husband, C. (1982) *Ethnic Relations and British Identity in Race and British Society*. Milton Keynes: Open University Press.

Husband, C. (1987) *'Race' in Britain: Continuity and Change*. London: Hutcheson.

Husband, C. (1994) *'Race' and Nation: the British Experience*. Perth: Paradigm Press.

Husband, C. (1995) The morally active practitioner and the ethics of anti-racist social work, in R. Hugman and D. Smith (eds) *Ethical Issues in Social Work*. London: Routledge.

Ineichen, B. (1989) Afro-Caribbeans and the incidence of schizophrenia: a review, *New Community*, 15(3), 335–41.

Jackson, P. and Penrose, J. (1993) *Constructions of Race, Place and Nation*. London: UCL Press.

Jenkins, R. and Solomos, J. (1989) *Racism and Equal Opportunities in the 1980s*. Cambridge: Cambridge University Press.

Jessop, B., Bonnett, K., Bromley, S. and Ling, T. (1988) *Thatcherism*. Cambridge: Polity Press.

Johnson, M. (1992) Health and Social Services, *New Community*, 18, 316–25.

Jones, C. (1993) Dishonesty, distortion and demonisation: the right and anti-racist social work education, *Social Work Education*, 12, 39–16.

Jones S. (1992) Improving retention and graduation rates for black students in nursing education: a developmental model, *Nursing Outlook*, 40(2), 79–85.

Jordan, W.D. (1969) *White over Black*. Harmondsworth: Penguin.

Joshua, H. and Wallace, T. (1983) *To Ride the Storm*. London: Heinemann.

Judge, K. and Solomon, M. (1993) Public opinion and the National Health Service: patterns and perspectives in consumer satisfaction, *Journal of Social Policy*, 22(3), 299–327.

Kareem, J. and Littlewood, R. (1992) *Intercultural Therapy*. Oxford: Blackwell Scientific Publications.

Karseras, P. and Hopkins, E. (1987) *British Asians' Health in the Community*. Chichester: John Wiley.

Kavanagh, K.H., Kennedy, P.H., Kohler, H.R., Rasin, J.H. and Schoen, D.C. (1993) Exploring the experience of African students in a school of nursing, *Journal of Nursing Education*, 32(6), 273–5.

Keith, M. and Pile, S. (1993) *Place and the Politics of Identity*. London: Routledge.

Kettle, M. and Hodges, L. (1982) *Uprising*. London: Pan Books.

Kiernan, V.G. (1969) *The Lords of Human Kind: European Attitudes to the Outside World in the Imperial Age*. London: Weidenfeld & Nicholson.

Kim, Y. (1989) Explaining interethnic conflict, in J. Gittler (ed.) *The Annual Review of Conflict Knowledge and Conflict Resolution*. New York: Garland.

Kim, Y.Y. (1992) Intercultural communication competence: a systems-theoretic view, in W.B. Gudykunst and Y.Y. Kim (eds) *Readings on Communication with Strangers*. New York: McGraw-Hill.

King Edward's Hospital Fund for London (1990) *Racial Equality: the Nursing Profession*. Equal Opportunities Task Force Occasional Paper No. 6. London: King's Fund Publishing Office.

Krueger, R.A. (1994) *Focus Groups*. London: Sage.

Lalljee, M. (1987) Attribution theory and intercultural communication, in K. Knapp, W. Enninger and A. Knapp-Polthoff (eds) *Analyzing Intercultural Communication*. New York: Mouton de Gruyter.

Lee Cumin, M. (1989) *Daughters of Seacole*. Batley: West Yorkshire Low Pay Unit.

Leininger, M. (1978) *Transcultural Nursing, Concepts, Theories and Practice*. New York: John Wiley.

Leininger, M. (1990) Ethnomethods: the philosophic and epistemic bases to explicate transcultural nursing knowledge, *Journal of Transcultural Nursing*, 1(2), 40–5.

Lynam, J. (1992) Towards the goal of providing culturally sensitive care: principles upon which to build nursing curricula, *Journal of Advanced Nursing*, 17, 149–57.

Mares, P., Henley, A. and Baxter, C. (1985) *Health Care in Multiracial Britain*. Cambridge: Health Care Education Council.

Marmot, M., Adelstein, A. and Bulusa, L. (1984) *Immigrant Mortality in England and Wales: 1970–1978*. London: HMSO.

Marshall, J.E. (1989) Student attrition: is lack of support a key?, *Nursing Outlook*, 37, 176–8.

Mason, D. (1986) Controversies and continuities in race and ethnic relations theory, in J. Rex and D. Mason (eds) *Theories of Race and Ethnic Relations*. Cambridge: Cambridge University Press.

McGee, P. (1992) *Teaching Transcultural Care*. London: Chapman & Hall.

McGee, P. (1994) Educational issues in transcultural nursing, *British Journal of Nursing*, 3(21), 1113–16.

McKeigure, P., Richards, J. and Richards, P. (1991) Effects of discrimination by sex and race on the early careers of British medical graduates during 1981–1987, *British Medical Journal*, 301, 961–4.

McNaught, A. (1994) A discriminating service: the socio-economic and scientific roots of racial discrimination in the National Health Service, *Journal of Interprofessional Care*, 8, 141–9.

Meekosha, H. (1993) The bodies politic – equality, difference and community practice, in H. Butcher, A. Glen, P. Henderson and J. Smith (eds) *Community and Public Policy*. London: Pluto Press.

Miles, R. (1989) *Racism*. London: Routledge.

Miles, R. and Phizacklea M. (1984) *White Man's Country: Racism in British Politics*. London: Pluto Press.

Modood, T. and Shiner, M. (1994) *Ethnic Minorities and Higher Education: Why Are There Differential Rates of Entry*. London: Policy Studies Institute.

Mohanty, C.T., Russo, A. and Torres, L. (1991) *Third World Women and the Politics of Feminism*. Bloomington: Indiana University Press.

Morgan, D.L. (ed.) (1993) *Successful Focus Groups*. London: Sage.

Morris, D. (1979) *Gestures*. London: Cape.

Murray, N. and Searle, C. (1989) *Racism and the Press in Thatcher's Britain*. London: Institute of Race Relations.

National Audit Office (1992) *Nursing Education: Implementation of Project 2000 in England*. London: HMSO.

National Health Service Executive (1995) *Non-medical Education and Training – Planning Guidance for 1996/97 Education Commissioning*. Ref EL(95)96. Annex. Leeds: National Health Service Executive.

Nursing Times (1995) Racism blamed for nurse shortage, *Nursing Times*, 91(19), 9.

Office of Population Censuses and Surveys (1992) *General Household Survey*. London: HMSO.

Papadopoulos, I., Tilki, M. and Alleyne, J. (1994a) Transcultural nursing and nurse education, *British Journal of Nursing*, 3(11), 583–6.

Papadopoulos, I., Alleyne, J. and Tilki, M. (1994b) Promoting transcultural care in a college of health care studies, *British Journal of Nursing*, 3(21), 1116–18.

Patel, N. (1990) *A 'Race' against Time*. London: Runnymede Trust.

Phizacklea, A. and Miles, R. (1980) *Labour and Racism*. London: Routledge and Kegan Paul.

Pilgrim, S., Fenton, S., Hughes, T., Hine, C. and Tibbs, N. (1993) *The Bristol Black and Ethnic Minorities Health Survey Report*. Bristol: University of Bristol.

Proctor, S. and Smith, I.J. (1992) A reconsideration of the factors affecting birth outcome in Pakistani Muslim families in Britain, *Midwifery*, 8, 76–81.

Rashid, A. (1990) Asian doctors and nurses in the NHS, in B.R. McVoy and L.J. Donaldson (eds) *Health Care for Asians*. Oxford: Oxford University Press.

Rex, J. (1986) *Race and Ethnicity*. Milton Keynes: Open University Press.

Rex, J. and Mason, D. (eds) (1986) *Theories of Race and Ethnic Relations*. Cambridge: Cambridge University Press.

Rex, J. and Tomlinson, S. (eds) (1979) *Colonial Immigrants in a British City*. London: Routledge and Kegan Paul.

Rich, P.B. (1990) *Race and Empire in British Politics*. Cambridge: Cambridge University Press.

Richardson, R.C. (1989) If minority students are to succeed in higher education, every rung of the education ladder must be in place, *The Chronicle of Higher Education*, 11 January, 15.

Roberts, C., Davies, E. and Jupp, T. (1992) *Language and Discrimination*. Harlow: Longman.

Rooney, B. (1987) *Racism and Resistance to Change*. Liverpool: Merseyside Area Profile Group.

Rose, E.J.B. (1969) *Colour and Citizenship*. London: Oxford University Press.

Ruben, B. and Kealey, D. (1979) Behavioural assessment of communication competency and the prediction of cross-cultural adaptation, *International Journal of Intercultural Relations*, 3, 15–48.

Said, H.M. (1983) The Unani system of health and medicare, in R.H. Bannerman, J. Burton, and C. Win-Chieh (eds) *Traditional Medicine and Health Care Coverage*. Geneva: World Health Organization.

Sashidharan, S.P. and Francis, E. (1993) Epidemiology, ethnicity and schizophrenia, in W.I.U. Ahmad (ed.) *'Race' and Health in Contemporary Britain*. Buckingham: Open University Press.

Shackman, J. (1985) *A Handbook of Working with Employing and Training Interpreters*. Cambridge: National Extension College.

Shah, S. (1989) Effective permeation of race and gender in teacher education courses, *Gender and Education*, 1(3), 231–6.

Sharma, K.M. (1990) Using alternative therapies: marginal medicine and central concerns, in P. Abbot and G. Payne (eds) *New Directions in the Sociology of Health*. London: Falmer Press.

Sheldon, T. and Parker, H. (1992) The use of 'ethnicity' and 'race' in health research: a cautionary note, in W.I.U. Ahmad (ed.) *The Politics of 'Race' and Health*. Bradford: Race Relations Research Unit, University of Bradford and Bradford and Ilkley Community College.

Sivanandan, A. (1981) RAT and the degradation of black struggle, *Race and Class*, 25(2), 1–33.

Skellington, R. (1992) *'Race' in Britain Today*. London: Sage.

Smaje, C. (1995) *Health, Race and Ethnicity: Making Sense of the Evidence*. London: King's Fund Institute.

Solomos, J. (1993) *Race and Racism in Britain*. London: Macmillan.

Stokes, G. (1991) A transcultural nurse is about, *Senior Nurse*, 11(1), 40–2.

Stone, M. (1981) *The Education of the Black Child in Britain*. London: Fontana.

Studlar, D.T. (1974) British public opinion, colour issues, and Enoch Powell: a longitudinal analysis, *British Journal of Political Science*, 4, 371–81.

Tajfel, H. (1978) *Differentiation between Social Groups*. London: Academic Press.

Torkington, N.P.K. (1987) Sorry wrong colour, *Nursing Times*, 83(24), 27–38.

Townsend, P. and Davidson, N. (1982) *Inequalities in Health: the Black Report*. Harmondsworth: Penguin.

Troyna, B. (1992) Can you see the join? An historical analysis of multicultural and antiracist education policies, in D. Gill, B. Mayor and M. Blair (eds) *Racism and Education*. London: Sage.

Troyna, B. and Williams, J. (1986) *Racism, Education and the State*. London: Croom Helm.

Turner, J.C. (1987) *Rediscovering the Social Group*. Oxford: Basil Blackwell.

Turner, J.C. and Giles, H. (1981) *Intergroup Behaviour*. Oxford: Basil Blackwell.

UKCC (1986) *Project 2000: a New Preparation for Practice*. London: UKCC.

UKCC (1989) *UKCC requirements for the Content of Project 2000 Programmes*. PS&D/89/04(B). London: UKCC.

van Dijk, T.A. (1991) *Racism and the Press*. London: Routledge.

Waldegrave, W. (1992) Foreword, in Commission for Racial Equality, *Race Relations Code of Practice in Primary Health Care Services*. London: Commission for Racial Equality.

Wallman, S. (1986) Ethnicity and the boundary process in context, in J. Rex and D. Mason (eds) *Theories of Race and Ethnic Relations*. Cambridge: Cambridge University Press.

Walvin, J. (1971) *The Black Presence*. London: Orback and Chambers.

Walvin, J. (1973) *Black and White: the Negro and English Society*. London: Allen Lane.

Ward, L. (1993) Race equality and employment in the National Health Service, in W.I.U. Ahmad (ed.) *'Race' and Health in Contemporary Britain*. Buckingham: Open University Press.

Weekes, D.P. (1989) Mentor–protégé relationships: a critical element in affirmative action, *Nursing Outlook*, 37(4), 156–7.

Whitehead, M. (1987) *The Health Divide*. London: Health Education Council.

Williams, J. (1985) Redefining institutional racism, *Ethnic and Racial Studies*, 8(3), 323–48.

Williams, J. and Rogers, S. (1993) The multi-cultural workplace: preparing preceptors, *Journal of Continuing Education in Nursing*, 24(3), 101–4.

Williams, T. (1995) *Chinese Medicine*. Shaftesbury: Element Books.

Wilson, M. (1994) *Healthy and Wise*. London: Virago.

Wrench, J. and Solomos, J. (1993) *Racism and Migration in Western Europe*. Oxford: Berg.

Yin, R.K. (1993) *Applications of Case Study Research*. Newbury Park, CA: Sage.

Yin, R.K. (1994) *Case Study Research: Design and Methods*, 2nd edn. Newbury Park, CA: Sage.

Index